Graham Handley and Stanley King

Brodie's Notes on Evelyn Waugh's

Scoop

Pan Books London and Sydney

First published 1980 by Pan Books Ltd
Cavaye Place, London SW10 9PG
1 2 3 4 5 6 7 8 9
© Graham Handley & Stanley King 1980
ISBN 0 330 50174 7
Filmset in Great Britain by
Northumberland Press Ltd, Gateshead, Tyne and Wear
Printed and bound by
Richard Clay (The Chaucer Press) Ltd, Bungay, Suffolk

Contents

The author and his work 5

Background and plot 9

Style 13

Characters 19

Section summaries and textual notes 27

Revision questions 79

Page references in these Notes are to the Penguin edition of *Scoop*, but as each chapter section is separately analysed, the Notes may be used with any edition of the book

To the student

A close reading of the set book is the student's primary task. These Notes will help to increase your understanding and appreciation of the novel, and to stimulate *your own* thinking about it. *The Notes are in no way intended as a substitute* for a thorough knowledge of the book.

The author and his work

Evelyn Waugh was born on 28 October 1903, the second son of
Arthur Waugh, a publisher who, in effect, ran the firm of Chapman
and Hall. Evelyn's brother was Alec Waugh, also to become a
writer, while on his father's side one of his relations was the critic
and writer Edmund Gosse; on his mother's he was in the direct
line from a famous judge, Lord Cockburn. The family lived at
North End, Hampstead, Evelyn going first to a private school at
Heath Mount until he was thirteen. At that time he should perhaps
have gone to Sherborne, but his brother Alec had been removed
from there in 1915, and Evelyn went to Lancing instead in 1917.
Some years prior to this, Evelyn had become interested in religion,
and his devotion to chapel was to remain with him for the rest
of his life. His brother Alec had written an account of life at
Sherborne in his *The Loom of Youth*, and Evelyn's parents were upset
by the publicity that accompanied the publication and reception
of this book. But life at Lancing improved for Evelyn with the
end of World War I in 1918, and he won an art prize at school
for an illuminated prayer. In fact for some time he entertained
the idea that he might become an artist, and he founded a society
that he called the Dilettanti, which was largely concerned with
debating. He even began a novel which was, however, abandoned
in 1921; in that year he again won a prize, this time for poetry.

At the end of 1921 Waugh sat a scholarship examination for
Hertford College, Oxford, and was successful. He went up to
Oxford in 1922, where he joined the Hypocrites Club, and had
a generally frivolous time. He was influenced by Harold Acton
(to whom he dedicated *Decline and Fall*) and Robert Byron, and
he came to know Cyril Connolly quite well. Evelyn always enjoyed
his drink and he further enjoyed, despite his own unpredictability
of behaviour, cultivating friendships. In 1924 he obtained his
degree, but it was a poor one. He then attended a school of fine
art, but did not find this experience an attractive one. Shortly afterwards he applied for a teaching job in Denbighshire, and much
of the narrative of his first novel *Decline and Fall* is attributable

to this experience, though the original Arnold House and its inmates bear perhaps but scant resemblance to Waugh's satirical account. He stayed a year and then went to another school, but made himself useful as a despatch rider during the General Strike of 1926.

Waugh toured Scotland, Greece and France with a friend, and after a privately-printed book on the pre-Raphaelite Brotherhood had achieved some notice, he was invited by the publisher Duckworth to write a biography of Rossetti. He also contributed to the *Daily Express* for a time, and earned some money by reviews. He met and proposed to Evelyn Gardner, whom he married in 1928. By that time he had finished *Decline and Fall*, which caused an immediate, largely favourable reaction through what Waugh's biographer Christopher Sykes calls quite correctly 'its perfect mingling of realism and fantasy'. This success led to greater opportunities, particularly in the field of journalism, but Waugh was soon at work on a new novel. His marriage foundered, and finally ended, but *Vile Bodies* was published in 1930, and from then on his success story, at least in terms of published work, takes its upward trend. The new novel sold well, and Waugh became established, the much-sought-after literary lion of the fashionable coteries.

In 1930 Waugh was received into the Roman Catholic Church; in the same year he visited Abyssinia – his third novel *Black Mischief* being one of the results of this trip. It enhanced his reputation as a largely comic novelist. In 1934 he published *A Handful of Dust*, with its somewhat bitter emphasis on the break-up of a marriage; there would appear to be an autobiographical element here. He published his study of the Catholic saint and martyr *Edmund Campion* in 1935, and it was awarded the Hawthornden Prize in 1936. His marriage had been annulled in 1935; there followed the publication of a book of stories in 1936; he married Laura Herbert in 1937. He wrote reviews for *The Spectator* and *Time and Tide*.

By November 1937 Waugh had completed *Scoop*, which was published in the following year when, incidentally, his first child was born. *Scoop*, the subject of this Study Aid, marks a happy return to the world of farce. He was not very active during the early part of 1939, but on the outbreak of war he found himself without employment and with heavy expenses involved with his delightful house Piers Court – though he did rent it to Dominican nuns during the war. He pressed for an appointment in the armed forces, and eventually got into the Marines. Later he was seconded to the Commandos, and later still played an important part in the Allied Military Mission to Yugoslavia. By the end of 1941 he had written *Put Out More Flags*; his fragment *Work Suspended* followed in 1942, which was, unusually for Waugh, written in the first person.

In 1943 Evelyn transferred to the Royal Horse Guards. *Brideshead Revisited* was published in 1945, and some critics have seen in its ample scope a debt to Thackeray, a writer and satirist much admired by Waugh. *Brideshead* was an enormous success; but Waugh's literary efforts for some time afterwards were in a noticeably minor key. The year 1947 saw the publication of *Scott-King's Modern Europe*; then Waugh visited the United States, the result of that visit being a small masterpiece on Californian commercialized burial practices: *The Loved One* (1948). In the next few years his friendship with the great Catholic and scholar Ronald Knox assumed an increasing importance. *Helena* came out in 1950 but, though highly valued by Waugh, was unfavourably reviewed by the critics. In 1951 Waugh was able to tell Graham Greene that he was engaged on 'an interminable novel about army life' – an early mention of the war trilogy on which his later more serious reputation was based. *Men at Arms*, the first part of the trilogy, was published in 1952, and in the next year followed a fantasy-nightmare called *Love Among the Ruins*, a strangely uncharacteristic offering, which Waugh himself described as a 'bit of nonsense'. (It is now published by Penguin Books in *The Ordeal of Gilbert Pinfold and Other Stories*, 1957.) The first, and longest, story in this collection, *The Ordeal of Gilbert Pinfold*, is somewhat autobiographical, one suspects. It is a compelling and very funny study in neurosis, though an air of pathos and the imminent sense of breakdown run through it. It seems as if Waugh suffered from melancholia and periodic doubts about his own sanity. Before that, *Officers and Gentlemen* (the second volume in the trilogy which goes under the title *Sword of Honour*), had appeared in 1955. Meanwhile Waugh had become friendly with Ian Fleming, the creator of James Bond.

In 1957 Ronald Knox died, and in 1959 Evelyn published a devoted biography of his great friend. In 1959–60 he was occupied with *Unconditional Surrender*, the third volume of the war trilogy *Sword of Honour*. Also in 1959, Waugh was offered the CBE, which he refused, as he appeared to think he was worthy of higher honours. In 1964 he published *A Little Learning*, an account of his early life, which the student is strongly recommended to read. Waugh was an abrasive character, often unpopular, obsessed about certain matters, and generally aggressive when he disliked either a person or a theory or both. *A Little Learning* sheds a new and somewhat warmer light on the author, who appears less exhibitionistic, more profoundly human than we might have thought.

In the last years of his life Waugh suffered from delusions; he died, silently and suddenly, in 1966. He left behind him work of considerable literary power, verve, wit, parody, fantasy: ironic and satiric fictions which, under the often sardonic gloss, have claims upon our serious attention. It is perhaps too early to say whether either the cynicism or the seriousness will survive the passage of time, but certainly Waugh must be accounted one of the finest novelists writing in English in the twentieth century.

Further reading

Other novels by Evelyn Waugh, particularly:

Decline and Fall (Heinemann Education, Penguin)

When the Going was Good (Penguin)

The Loved One (Chapman & Hall, Penguin)

A Little Learning, Evelyn Waugh's Autobiography
(Sidgwick & Jackson, New English Library)

The Diaries of Evelyn Waugh, Ed. by Michael Davis
(Weidenfeld & Nicolson)

Evelyn Waugh, Christopher Hollis
(Longman's for British Council)

Evelyn Waugh; A Biography, Christopher Sykes (Collins)

Background and plot

Background

For a thorough understanding of the background to *Scoop*, the student would do well to read Evelyn Waugh's *When the Going was Good* (first published in 1946, still available in the Penguin edition). From 1928 to 1937 Waugh spent his time travelling, and writing about his travels. *When the Going was Good* is a condensed and very amusing account of those travels, containing all that he wished to preserve. The first section covers his pleasure cruise to the Middle East in 1929, and is full of anecdotes about the various places visited, notably Egypt, Malta and Greece. The next section, 'A Coronation in 1930', has somewhat closer connections with *Scoop*, since it deals with the ceremonies attendant upon the crowning of the Emperor of Abyssinia. Again the factual and the amusing vie for pre-eminence in what is both an entertaining and an interesting piece of writing.

It is with the last section of *When the Going was Good* (extracts from *Waugh in Abyssinia*), that we are most concerned; students of *Scoop* will recognize the irony here of such phrases as 'knowledgeable discrimination at the tropical outfitters', and realize that William at least did not possess any. Waugh refers to one of his fellow journalists as saying that 'the Emperor was an oppressed anti-fascist' – which echoes the political manoeuvring in Jacksonburg as reporters buzz in that capital like the flies on Frau Dressler's milch-goat. Moreover, the original of Baldwin surely appears in *When the Going was Good* as the gentleman who 'suddenly, to become world-famous ... spoke more freely about a pack of hounds which he had in the Midlands, and when, as often happened, he received lengthy cables in code, he would pocket them, nonchalantly, remarking, "From my huntsman. He says the prospects for cubbin' are excellent."' Waugh also refers to the meetings of the Foreign Press Association as 'acrimonious', and one such meeting occurs in *Scoop*.

The cables in *When the Going was Good* have a marked resemblance to those in *Scoop*; for example '*Require earliest name life story photograph*

American nurse upblown Adowa' together with the graphic reply '*Nurse unupblown*'. There are various other marked parallels, which the interested student can easily investigate, and a piece of typical Waugh irony in 'There were a number of journalists there reporting the war at leisure from their imaginations.' In a sense *Waugh in Abyssinia* is to *Scoop* what Graham Greene's *The Lawless Roads: Mexico* is to his *The Power and the Glory*: the documentary that precedes the fiction; the source that fertilizes the imagination.

Christopher Sykes, in his fine biography of Waugh (Penguin, 1977) provides even more detail about the background: Waugh was sent out to Abyssinia in August 1935 as war correspondent of the *Daily Mail*; he was known to be pro-Italian in his views, and was for some time thought to be an Italian spy. Meanwhile the British government – led by Stanley Baldwin – was, according to Sykes, 'busy propagating the notion that Britain was the stainless champion of Abyssinia against the aggression and economic greed of Italy'. Waugh discovered that the Italians were about to attack Abyssinia within two weeks of 18 September 1935, but knowing that this cable would be sold or intercepted he apparently sent it to the *Daily Mail* in Latin. The sub-editor did not print it, and the result was that the *Mail* lost a scoop and Evelyn received a reprimand for wasting the paper's time and money. He later resigned, and his assignment was given to another. Early in 1936 he had an interview with Mussolini, the Italian Fascist dictator, with whom he was apparently very impressed.

The student will need to know something of the factual background to the events described by Waugh. Mussolini had come to power in 1922, and soon began to inject an assertiveness into Italian foreign affairs. Italy had always been jealous of the French colonial empire and had colonial aspirations of her own. Mussolini sought to elevate Germany – despite her defeat in World War I (1914–18) – and he succeeded in welcoming Germany into the League of Nations in 1926. In 1933 he proposed a Four-Power Pact between Italy, Germany, Great Britain and France, which would liaise on matters of foreign and colonial policy; it would also allow Germany the right to rearm if the other powers failed to disarm. Basically, and tragically, this was instrumental in bringing about World War II in 1939.

Before then, however, Italy and Germany almost clashed over the determination of each to control Austria – Hitler wanting it as part of Germany while Italy regarded Austria as a threat to her Northern frontier. Italy thus drew closer to France. But when Germany began to rearm, although the League of Nations condemned her, the League took no direct action against Hitler. Mussolini did not want conflict with Hitler at this time, since he was preparing to take over Abyssinia, which was an independent state situated between Italian Somaliland and Eritrea. Italy had tried to seize Abyssinia as early as 1896, but had been defeated at the battle of Adowa. Mussolini had tried by friendly means to gain influence over Abyssinia, but by 1935 he had reached an agreement with France that allowed for a degree of Italian influence in Abyssinia. In October 1935 Mussolini invaded Abyssinia, and found that none of the great powers was prepared to go to war against him. The League of Nations imposed ineffectual sanctions against Italy, but in 1936 she conquered Abyssinia. The Emperor Haile Selassie fled, and Italy left the League of Nations, having demonstrated just how impotent that body was.

Plot

Although there are many, and varied characters in *Scoop*, the basic plot is relatively clear in outline. John Courteney Boot, novelist, distantly related to the Boots of Boot Magna, is anxious to get a good journalistic assignment, and approaches the influential socialite Mrs Stitch to help him. She does so by getting Lord Copper, newspaper magnate, to promote the name Boot through his editor Mr Salter. But the wrong Boot is approached: William is already employed by the *Beast* to write a column on *Lush Places* and has made an unfortunate error in the previous week's issue. Summoned to London, he is fearful that he is in for a reprimand, but instead finds himself assigned to Ishmaelia where a news story is about to break.

This is against all William's instincts, but he travels to Ishmaelia; in the course of a somewhat hectic trip, he meets an impressive and obviously wealthy man (later to be known as Baldwin), who does not reappear until later in the story. He also makes the acquaintance of Corker, another journalist. Arrived in Ishmaelia, William meets many other journalists, from many countries, also assigned to the Ishmaelia 'story'. He finds Ishmaelia to be a hotbed of political intrigue and duplicity; it is a kind of playground for the major powers and international financiers. There are a number of incidents, many of them farcical; William meets and falls in love with Kätchen.

Through the influence of Dr Benito (the Ishmaelian Minister of Foreign Affairs and Propaganda), all the journalists are got out of the way up-country; William alone stays. His earlier travelling acquaintance Mr Baldwin now appears, and William acquires fuller details of the story he had earlier received from Kätchen and which had provided him with his first 'scoop'. Through the cunning and organization of Baldwin, who enlists the aid of Olaf Eriksen (with murderous effect), the Communists' coup d'état through Benito is overthrown. William's early despatches are enhanced by a superbly sophisticated one from Baldwin in William's name. William of course has 'scooped' the world, and returns to find himself famous. Before that Kätchen's 'husband' has reappeared from the interior, so when William says goodbye to her, his romance is over.

When William returns to England a banquet is arranged by Lord Copper for *Boot of the Beast* and Mr Salter (after enduring the agonies of arriving at Boot Magna), gets William's coveted signature. There now occurs a dual mistake in identity, just to make confusion worse confounded: John Boot is knighted in error for William; his lecherous Uncle Theodore supplants William at the banquet and enjoys the fruits of his success. William retires to Boot Magna, comfortable for life, and continues to write *Lush Places*. The wheel of his fortune has come full circle; he has 'scooped' the world's best journalists but the quiet course of his life, despite a nostalgic recall of Jacksonburg at the height of his romance with Kätchen, has remained unchanged.

Style

The style of *Scoop* is basically one of satire, humour and farce – largely political and journalistic farce, as distinct from that standby of the theatre, bedroom farce. Style and plot are intimately linked in *Scoop* with, for example, Mrs Stitch's drive into the gentlemen's lavatory being a stitch in the plot but also an early instance of Waugh's farcical verve. The ridiculousness of this situation underlining the overall nonsense of the situation we are later to find in Ishmaelia. The sub-title ('A novel about journalists') hardly indicates the range of the satire, which not only embraces Fleet Street and some of its giant newspapers, with their calculated unconcern for truth (only the sensational is saleable), but also takes a close look at various aspects of the society of the time. We may marvel today at the unchanging truth of *Scoop* (the title too is an excellent condensation of the focus of the novel and its puppets): Waugh knew from experience that the press (with notable exceptions) must cater for man's basic instincts – hence his choice of such names as the *Beast* and the *Brute*.

In fact one of the major facets of Waugh's style is his penchant for names (see Textual Notes) that would have had much meaning for his contemporaries. The name of a leading left-wing publisher of the thirties is given to an establishment general in Ishmaelia; the Director of the Press Bureau in that country has the same first name as the infamous Italian dictator of the time, Benito Mussolini, who was later to be the ally of Hitler in World War II.

Mrs Stitch has her own tightly-knit function in the intrigue, but drops an important stitch with hilarious results that negatively involve John Courteney Boot, and, positively, William throughout, also, at the end, the unshakeable and lecherous Uncle Theodore. It is not our intention here to over-stress Waugh's use of names, since the Textual Notes will supply the essential guidance and flavour of his intentions and emphases. But the alert student must be aware that this packed novel depends for much of its effect on contemporary reference and, occasionally, on in-jokes that are now difficult to understand. But one aspect of Waugh's style that is certainly satirical is his ability to poke oblique fun not only at the cruder and more unscrupulous aspects of journalism but also at his fellow writers. Uncle Theodore is something of a Wodehousian character, while the succession of bedridden nannies and servants constitutes almost a group of semi-refined above-stairs equivalents of the Starkadders of Stella Gibbons's *Cold Comfort Farm*.

Scoop is written with such verve that it takes in the literary as well as the political scene, and its greatest asset is the sustained quality and range of its humour. From the first page that humour, with its tongue-in-cheek view of the writings of John Courteney Boot (not unlike the writings of the young Evelyn Waugh incidentally) and its description of a 'biting cold mid-June morning' indicates that Waugh intends, like Mrs Stitch, to turn convention on its head. When John Boot meets Mrs Stitch, a typically evocative Waugh simile enhances the description of her – 'her normally mobile face encased in clay was rigid and menacing as an Aztec mask' (p.6) – while the whole scene, with child prodigy, maid, and the elegant young man who is painting ruined castles on the ceiling is in the lightly-etched Waugh vein of running satire. Once Julia Stitch opens her mouth Waugh's satire embraces society speech and the activities of the do-gooders of that society ('Why should I go to Viola Chasm's Distressed Area; did she come to my Model Madhouse?').

So rich is the humour, so thickly inlaid is the text, that one is apt to miss the casual aside, like the one about Lady Metroland's footman being on a diet. If society speech is satirized, then pompous and pretentious speech (witness Lord Copper) receives even more severe treatment. In fact Lord Copper is cocooned in humour, particularly through his subordinate, Mr Salter, who vacillates between 'Definitely' and 'Up to a point' when talking to the Megalopolitan magnate. The newspaper satire begins in earnest with the superbly inept though alliterative '*Feather-footed through the plashy fens passes the questing vole*' (p.21), a send-up of the 'literary' countryman's column in a newspaper.

The influence of P. G. Wodehouse is certainly seen in the initial description of Boot Magna Hall, and what is being satirized here is decayed (and in some cases decadent) gentry, the keeping-on of old retainers who retain themselves. This is developed through a humorous account of each, their relationships, and the interminable marathon eating that supposedly characterizes the servants' hall. In contrast – and Waugh is a master of contrast – there is the materialistic ostentation of Copper House with its 'Byzantine vestibule and Sassanian lounge' together with the 'series of girls in Caucasian uniform'. This sustained emphasis pictures a synthetic society as distinct from William's ancestral background and the essential simplicity of his mind. Salter's first conversations with William embody conventional satire of the townee and his attitude towards anyone up from the country, e.g. 'Lot of foot and mouth I expect' (p.27) and 'I expect you feel like a drop of zider about this time' (p.28). Here we come to another facet of Waugh's stylistic talent – he has a natural flair for dialogue that exactly captures both the humorous and the commonplace in conversational exchanges, as in Salter's remark to William, which gives us some indication of the political climate of the time: 'You see, he's a communist. Most of the staff of the *Twopence* are – they're University men, you see' (p.32). Their conversation is also a comedy of situation, with William unaware of his own potential money-earning capacity as the up-and-coming foreign correspondent in Ishmaelia.

Basic human psychology is exposed to the various verbal thrusts of Waugh; he also has a Dickensian propensity towards caricature and the grotesque – for example, the midget who waits upon William after his night in town is called 'a page with a face of ageless evil'. In a novel which, as he has said, is fundamentally about journalists, Waugh himself captures journalistic economy with a rare hilarity; the first slip which William reads merely says, '*Mrs Stitch. Gentlemen's Lavatory, Sloane Street*', and that cryptic message is a prelude to William's first experience of the tenacity of newshounds with the sensational within their jaws. This also reveals the depth at which Waugh works, for when Mrs Stitch says, 'It's simply a case of mistaken identity,' she sounds the note that is to be fully orchestrated later in the plot – namely the mistaken identity that sends William into Ishmaelia and Uncle Theodore to a place of honour next to Lord Copper at the celebration banquet for 'Boot of the *Beast*'.

Throughout the novel we note the economy of the imagery, whether it be lightly irreverent ('their keys made no more sound than the drumming of a bishop's fingertips on an upholstered prie-dieu') or sheerly imaginative ('the telephone buzzers were muffled and purred like warm cats'). Once William is launched on the mission (though he has no idea of the geographical or moral directions in which he is going) Waugh's satire acquires a sharper and more biting edge, having a realistic basis in the events of the time ('of course, it's really a war between Russia and Germany and Italy and Japan').

A good example of Waugh's use of caricature is the first description of General Cruttwell FRGS, and the clever innuendo that follows concerning the fictional and useless paraphernalia of cleft sticks, tiffin gun, a set of chota pegs and a chota mallet, even down to the astrolabe and the portable humidor. Here Waugh is guying what might be called the 'racket' in tropical gear. The delay in the issue of William's passport enables Waugh to satirize the kind of public and political oratory that can still be heard in Hyde Park (at Speaker's Corner); the press reportage of Mrs Stitch's escapade ('Society Beauty in Public Convenience'); and the hole-in-the-wall situation of the Ishmaelite Legation ('If away leave letters with tobacconist at No 162'). But there is acid beneath the fun; it burns through in the account of the Communist legation and its rival Nazi one ('A gold swastika on a white ground'), where the black official claims to be 'pure Aryan'.

William's trip is punctuated by caricature-nonsensical conversations in French, and his acquaintance, who knows everything (and has everything) is satirized in a succession of wealth-symbol possessions (e.g. a cabochon emerald, a coroneted crêpe-de-chine handkerchief), and of course all the right associations, English as well as international ('We march with the Fernie ... I long for my little house at Antibes'). The variation in Waugh's tone is remarkable; when William sees the white fish he dreams lyrically of trout and composes part of his imaginary column on *Lush Places*. With the arrival of Corker Waugh is able to switch his mockery of continentals to a like mockery of the Englishman abroad ('Hi, you, Alphonse, comprenez pint of bitter?'); this in turn is extended to further satire of the journalists with a nose for a story, which sometimes gets on the wrong scent – as with Corker's comforting of the wrong widow in East Sheen whose husband suddenly arrived back and 'cut up very nasty'.

Corker's anecdotes about Fleet Street contain some of Waugh's most cutting analysis of the way 'news' is fabricated ('the luscious, detailed inventions that composed contemporary history'); it is surely no accident that one of the most legendary journalists is called Wenlock Jakes, whose reportage of a fake war won him the Nobel Peace Prize for his 'harrowing descriptions of the carnage' which was, of course, non-existent.

As they near Ishmaelia, and when they arrive, Waugh's style is imbued with a cryptic ironic humour which consists of parodying news agency telegrams, all of which contrast with the style in which William sends his, naive and verbose by comparison with Corker's superb 'Aden Unwarwise'. The telling thing here is of course Waugh's ability to establish the 'in' lingo – a corruption of language, just as the 'news' reported is a corruption of the truth.

Ishmaelia itself provides the central political satire, heavy irony used in portraying the establishment of the Jacksonian line and its self-perpetuation of power, all descendant Jacksons bearing the satirical burden of having Waugh's names foisted on them (from Samuel Smiles to Huxley). Naturally, Ishmaelia is a member of the League of Nations, that ineffectual organization for the maintenance of peace after World War I; the White Shirt movement is equivalent to the Fascist Black Shirt movement of the 1930s, and the complexity of Ishmaelite politics reflects in a small (and transparently untrue way) the major political maelstroms of the time.

The whole of Book 2, 'Stones £20', is full of satirical overtones in the style. Wenlock Jakes, for example, is writing *Under the Ermine*; the French journalists are insecure and caricatured; the status and position of Erik Olafsen is established (again the ridicule is apparent), while the rainy season is defined in the poetic and economic 'And the granite sky wept' which opens Section 3, P. Shumble's scoop and its repercussions provides another form of humour in the volley of telegrams it provokes. Equally amusing, though with a sardonic overtone, is the kind of official communique issued by Gabriel Benito, almost a kind of parody of the hypocritical denial issued from time to time by the large nations in the international power game played so often and so riskily in the 1930s.

The references to *Garbo* and *Bergner*, the Pension *Dressler*, and the presence of the inevitable camera crew, all bring in the film motif. The film associations are further kept up by the introduction of Kätchen, and William's predictably falling in love with her.

Before this occurs there is a hilarious, totally farcical meeting of the Foreign Press Association – which, inevitably perhaps, degenerates into a series of private squabbles, conveyed by Waugh in snatches of dialogue. Private idiom here breaks the barriers of frustration, but this is knockabout comedy, another example of the variety of Waugh's humour and of the range and control he employs in the novel; the tempo never flags.

As we have seen, Waugh constantly employs contrast, but this is sometimes heightened too by a repetition of events: e.g. Erik Olafsen's account of his murderous action in the past prepares the reader for his single-handed murderous action in the present which overcomes the Communist coup d'état with ridiculous ease.

Consider the running comedy of all the references to Popotakis's ping-pong parlour, a kind of 'Peter Piper picked' alliteration that adds to its ridiculousness as a social or recreational centre. William's cables are not only literary, they are also funny, especially when he notes that the weather is improving though bubonic plague is raging. But his 'moment of history' is expertly and economically chronicled, for he notes the alliance of Benito and the Russian Jew while, as Waugh puts it, his fellow journalists up country are stranded like Noah and his ark. The duplicity of the plague rumour is cunningly underlined by Waugh in one of the most farcical scenes of all (he is laying clues about the coming coup d'état), i.e. when the milch-goat vanquishes 'the welter-weight champion of the Adventist University of Alabama'. William's momentous despatch is not allowed to go unsatirized: 'The keys rose together like bristles on a porcupine ... curious anagrams appeared on the paper before him.

Waugh is, supremely, an entertaining novelist, master of verbal humour, farce, fun, situation comedy, irony and, above all, satire. He makes economical and telling use of imagery and dialogue, heightened by contrast, caricature, the grotesque, parody and burlesque. He is a verbal craftsman embracing the wider ranges of humour.

Characters

Scoop is rich in characters or, more accurately, caricatures. The nature of this novel does not allow for or require treatment of the human personality in depth, and part of the fun lies in the fact that the *variety* of the characterization provides some of the most stimulating contrasting effects. Consider William as the natural antithesis of Lord Copper, or Mr Salter as the opposite of Uncle Theodore.

William Boot

The work was of the utmost importance to him: he was paid a guinea a time and it gave him the possible excuse for remaining uninterruptedly in the country.

William is the archetype of the 'innocent abroad'. The shy, diffident, rather withdrawn, country-loving hero of the book, lives in reasonable content in so far as he can do so in his Nannie-ridden mansion, while sending his weekly article on *Lush Places* to the *Beast*. Thanks to the machinations of Mrs Stitch, William is caught up in the web of mistaken identity upon which the plot turns. He is apprehensive about going to London, more apprehensive still when sucked into the whirl of Mr Salter's entertainment; he is naive and open to exploitation either by pages who are midgets or foreign girls with the Garbo look. He is romantic, gullible, totally unfitted to be a reporter (after all, he is dangerously liable to tell the truth).

William is the foil, rather than the butt, of Waugh's satire. He always has our sympathy and affection, but the idea of his actually obtaining the scoop is – if we stop to think about it – ludicrous, since he displays his ignorance of journalistic sharp practice at every turn. He is singularly, one suspects permanently, unversed in the ways of the world. On the other hand, it is William's simplicity and honesty that makes him reject Benito's schemes for getting the journalists out of town, so that he is the only journalist left in Jacksonburg and in a position, with the help of the sophisticated

Baldwin (who is perhaps attracted by William's innocence) to achieve his scoop. – which no doubt serves Baldwin's own ends too.

William remains innocent and thoroughly likeable to the end, but the word 'sucker' used of him is unkind and not entirely true. He is trusting and amiable up to a point, but if his would-be exploiters (Kätchen, for instance; Benito, or Lord Copper with his banquet) go too far, the reader is aware of a stiffening of William's backbone, and the aggressor retreats.

William's story is an allegory: that of the man who has succeeded through innocence, then turns away from corruption and back to the simple life he loves.

Mr Salter

Mr Salter's ultimate ambition was to take charge of the Competitions. Meanwhile he was Foreign Editor and found it a dog's life.

Salter, unlike William, is a true victim. A former editor of the Woman's page, which he had enjoyed, he now finds himself caught up in the directives of Lord Copper, merely uttering his 'Definitely' if he thinks Lord Copper right, and 'Up to a point' if he thinks him wrong. William is Mr Salter's responsibility, and at first he treats him as a country bumpkin, for what can he – Salter of Welwyn Garden City – know of rural life? But after the 'Garge' and the 'zider' gambits, Salter finds that William is after all human and relatively normal; they share a like diffidence and uncertainty, and Salter finds himself in the awkward position of initiating William into a life which he (Salter) despises – the life of sophisticated, competitive, corrupt journalism in which the word of men like Lord Copper and Lord Zinc passes for law. Because of this Salter is forced to adopt a reverential, or at best a compromising, attitude towards Lord Copper whom, anyway, he feels he does not really know. He explains to William exactly what Lord Copper requires from his reportage in Ishmaelia ('Lord Copper only wants Patriot victories') and this of courses underlines the fact that Salter has sold himself to his boss.

Salter lives on his nerves, witness his reaction when William's passport is delayed. But once William is in Ishmaelia, Salter leads a dog's life, although for most of the narrative we hear little of him; William's despatches, couched in an abbreviated literary form of the language of *Lush Places*, are sufficiently disconcerting: 'RAINING HARD HOPE ALL WELL ENGLAND' (p.121). He is particularly put out by the 'weather improving' after William has been in Jacksonburg for ten days, and this even causes him to question Lord Copper's judgement in sending William out there. Salter is forced into the cabling game himself, even sacking William before the 'scoop' arrives. Following this desirable turn of revelations, Salter's faith is restored, and he has reluctantly to acknowledge, that 'Lord Copper knows best'.

Salter gives way on the question of William's proposed knighthood; William's return marks an increase in Salter's worries. He is appalled when he discovers that the wrong Boot is to be knighted, has to conceal the fact from Lord Copper, and determines to go to Boot Magna. Here Salter is 'victim' indeed: his first encounter at the station with boy and slag; his long walk, so exhausting him that the Boots think he is drunk; his treatment at the hands of various members of the Boot family (being forced to look after Amabel, being button-holed by Uncle Theodore etc.). Admittedly he gets William's signature to the contract, but loses twenty-two shillings to Nannie Price (and endures much sexual innuendo from her).

Fortunately for Salter Uncle Theodore saves the day by substituting for William at the banquet. And Salter finally gets what he needs and deserves: he becomes art editor of *Home Knitting*, gaining 'punctual domestic dinners; Sunday at home among the crazy pavements'. He is a sympathetic and suffering character, something akin to William, but his lush places are in Welwyn Garden City, with regular Ovaltine.

Lord Copper

Lord Copper sat alone in splendid tranquillity. His massive head, empty of thought, rested in sculptural fashion upon his left fist. He began to draw a little cow upon his writing pad.

Lord Copper is the Megalopolitan Magnate, the self-made provincial whose subordinates tremble at his every word: he makes and breaks them. He is dazzled by Mrs Stitch; bullies Salter; determines policy and statements (in fact makes the news, which is not fact but policy); has ghastly ostentatious taste in buildings and accessories, is inadequate as an individual. This inadequacy is never exposed, for no one would dare to expose it; the error of 'which' Boot is perpetuated through Lord Copper's ignorance, so he ends up almost believing that Uncle Theodore is the Boot of the *Beast* for whom the banquet and his own long speech is given. Lord Copper is the master of platitude and misjudgement, the object of the author's satire of the ill-informed, ignorant but pretentious and powerful newspaper baron. In reality he is a sad and lonely figure, enjoying the exercise of speech-making but intractable when it comes to being crossed in argument (witness Sir Jocelyn Hitchcock). He is caricature of a grotesque kind, almost Dickensian in the flamboyant distortion of his portrayal.

Mrs Stitch

He knew of Mrs Stitch; from time to time he had seen her in the distance; now for the first time he found himself riddled through and through, mesmerized, inebriated. Those at the table, witnessing the familiar process, began to conjecture in tones which Lord Copper was too much entranced to overhear, what Julia could possibly want of him.

Although the actual space she occupies in the book is small, no one could call Mrs Stitch a minor character. She is a beautiful, mercurial, highly intelligent society woman, with a finger in numerous pies. She interferes, with the kindest intentions, in the affairs of others – and it is due to one such interference that William's life is, at least temporarily, greatly changed.

When the book opens, John Boot (William's distant relation) is visiting Mrs Stitch: 'Like all in her circle John Boot habitually brought his difficulties to her for solution.' He finds her still in bed, though it is 11 a.m. Her face is stiff with a clay beauty mask, but this does not prevent her from dictating to her secretary, doing (with her maid) the daily crossword, helping her daughter with her Latin homework, speaking on the telephone, and supervising the work of the elegant young man who is painting castles on her bedroom ceiling. She welcomes John, then adds, 'You can come and buy carpets with me; I've found a new shop in Bethnal Green, kept by a very interesting Jew who speaks no English; the most extraordinary things keep happening to his sister' (p.7).

She and John set off in her baby car, which she usually drives on the pavement when frustrated by heavy traffic: '... a policeman took her number and ordered her into the road ... "Third time this week," said Mrs Stitch. "I wish they wouldn't"' (p.9). It is on this drive that Julia promises to try to get John a posting to Ishmaelia for the *Beast*.

Julia Stitch has all the self-confidence of her beauty and her upper-class position in society; it is her idiosyncratic driving habits that finally land her so ludicrously at the Gentlemen's Lavatory in Sloane Street – the only time William ever sees her: '... the most beautiful woman William had ever seen ... chatting in a composed and friendly manner to the circle of reporters and plain-clothes men ... "I've a *great* deal to do. I do think some of you might help, instead of standing there asking questions"' (p.40).

Baldwin

He was a small man in a hurry, yet, bustling and buttoned up as he was, a man of unmistakable importance, radiating something of the dignity of a prize Pekingese.

'Baldwin' (the name William finally learns to call him by, though at their first meeting is just a mysterious stranger) travels to Le Bourget with the unwilling newspaper correspondent. He is obviously used to commanding respect and authority, is polite and knowledgeable, cultured and intelligent, suave and important at one and the same time, and speaks a number of languages. William meets him again on the train from Paris. He is heavily-jewelled; talks in a voice that seems to be a blend of a number of races, though he continually stresses his 'Englishness'; has many homes, from Marseilles and Antibes to his 'little pack of hounds in the Midlands'. He is sophisticated and charming; cosmopolitan and conservative; the mystery man of the mystery novel: presented with remarkable restraint and adroitness by Waugh.

We do not believe in 'Baldwin': he is too consummately polished, as international manipulators and financiers often are. William does not see him again until there is a passport check on the *Francmaçon*; Corker sees Baldwin as a 'pansy'. Baldwin is now equipped with a Costa Rican passport; he is, to use William's word, enigmatic. In the best tradition of mystery men he arrives at the crisis of events in Jacksonburg by parachute, cunningly enlists the help of Olafsen, explains the complications of international intrigue and finance to William, ensures that his second scoop is bigger and better than his first, and puts his seal upon it by vastly improving and explicitly emphasizing the finer points of his own superb control of the situation.

We have to refer to Waugh's *When the going was good* for Baldwin's original, if indeed there is an original of such a complex though stereotypically fictional character. He excels at everything he touches: from ping-pong to finance; from politics to its natural collateral activity, intrigue. Above all he is, beneath that suave and unruffled exterior, both cunning and persuasive.

Corker

'Anyone mind if I park myself here?'

Corker is the Englishman abroad: patronizing; rude; intent on collecting curios and thus showing that he has no taste. His career has prospered since he was lucky enough to get the story of a knight's widow whose foot is trapped between lift and landing (rather like the plight of Mrs Stitch), but he talks in cliché and jargon, regards William as suspect (until he finds that they are working on the same side), strikes up a friendship with Pigge out of self-interest, and has the difficult function in the novel of explaining the ways of the newspaper world to William. He instructs him in cable-ese, interprets that (to William) difficult language, notes how quickly and romantically William falls in love, suspects Shumble of having a scoop, loses his curios and recovers some, has no idea of what they are worth, and is foolish enough to set off for Laku and get stuck. Corker is not a corker: he has plenty of fizz but no natural aptitude – on the other hand, he does have a tendency to bounce to the surface after vicissitudes. But, from the time that he eats the bad fish and develops nettle-rash he makes blunder upon blunder. He is the major caricature among the journalists in terms of sheer foolishness.

Kätchen

A straggle of damp gold hair clung to her cheek. She wore red gum boots, shiny and wet, spattered with the mud of the streets. Her mackintosh dripped on the linoleum ... Garbo

Kätchen provides a further emphasis of Waugh's use of the essentially cinematic association in *Scoop*. Whether she really looks like Garbo doesn't matter; Waugh is guying the character of the lost romantic heroine by placing this one in the ideal romantic situation – alone, unfriended, penniless – thus making her a part of William's education. She is also, through her 'husband', part of the German plot in the area; she is an efficient 'gold-digger', uses William – but not without warmth and pathos. And she provides him with that taste of love he needs, to compensate for his (temporary) abandonment of *Lush Places*. She not only initiates William in the act of love, she also provides a practical explanation of the expense account by appropriating most of it herself once she has made inroads into William's susceptible heart. Where the cinema would have made her unblemished and innocent (by the then Hollywood code) Waugh makes her blemished – though, as Corker observes, she is 'winsome'. She is appealing to the reader as well as to William; the variety of her moods – and the poor quality of her acting – make her attractive and funny. The unscrupulousness that underlines her attitudes is demonstrated but not explicitly stated by Waugh.

Other characters

Since Waugh works basically at caricature level, the student should note the main facets of the minor characters mentioned here by simple investigation. They tend to fall into easily recognizable groups.

Uncle Theodore dominates Boot Magna, with his rich past in Paris and London as yet unwritten but constantly referred to. He is an old lecher of remarkable stamina, exulting in his own wickedness;

he is forever on the prowl, and contrasts with William by the outgoing nature of his salacious personality. His big moment is the banquet, his leers acting as a commentary on Lord Copper's apparent uprightness.

Nannie Bloggs, *Nannie Price* and *Priscilla* also have marked characteristics sketched in with considerable verve, and the geriatric group here are deftly presented in their own idiosyncratic colours.

Boot Magna is a long step geographically to Jacksonburg, where the journalists' names are almost self-explanatory: *Shumble*, *Whelper*, *Pigge*; their senior colleagues around whom sensation and fiction revolve are Jakes and Hitchcock, both of them individualized, but only at a superficial level. They are journalists straight out of some film, just as *Erik Olafsen* is the film-berserk man calculated to play his part in the grotesque climax. One would like to think that Waugh is satirizing too the distinct interest in psychology, that riddled the thirties with character interpretation – as indeed it does today.

Paleologue is a superb 'jackal', the man who always turns a particular situation to advantage, while *Frau Dressler* and *Mrs Earl Russell Jackson* have their own individual eccentricities: Frau Dressler's being largely devoted to the space under her bed, Mrs Jackson's to her dignity and the ache in her sit-upon.

Moke Bannister, while friendly and useful to William, is really no more than the caricature diplomat lost in a backwater abroad (though we note the old-school-tie influence).

Then there are the composite groups, like *the minor journalists* and *Benito and his Adventist Mission representative*. Waugh has a flair for providing what his journalists would call 'colour'; his characters, however brief their appearances, live positively in the context he has created for them.

Section summaries and textual notes

Book 1 *The Stitch Service*
Chapter 1

Section 1

John Courteney Boot, member of a minor offshoot of an obscure and impoverished county family, but famous in a modest way in his own right as an author, wants to get away from a romantic entanglement. He seeks the advice of Mrs Algernon Stitch, a lovely woman of formidable intelligence, great charm and iron will; he finds her – still in bed at past eleven in the morning – carrying on a number of conversations on various subjects at the same time. Mrs Stitch invites John to accompany her on a car journey to farthest Bethnal Green, and in one of the innumerable traffic jams of London 1936/7 he notices a newspaper placard referring to Ishmaelia. Mrs Stitch instantly sees that here is a way out for him, and promises to speak to Lord Copper (proprietor of the newspaper the *Beast*), whom she is meeting at lunch that day. This opening section conveys an impression of a great London hostess and the sort of society which she adorns and in which she moves – a society largely given to various entertainments in the name of charity, which afford endless opportunities for backbiting and outdoing one's friends. Further, the section, with its descriptions of delays and disruptions, prepares us for the fate that awaits our humble hero William.

Section 2

At the home of another great hostess, Lady Metroland. Mrs Stitch dazzles Lord Copper with her beauty and charm, and skilfully plants the idea that John Boot is just the man Lord Copper should send to Ishmaelia as a foreign correspondent. She is backed by her friends, and this bit of jobbery is apparently settled. Note how Lord Copper is revealed as a man devoted to the belief that newspaper owners are the true servants of the public; he is carried away by his own oratory. His power of patronage is revealed, and this contrasts with Mrs Stitch's skilful management.

Section 3

Mr Salter, the unwilling occupier of the post of foreign editor of the *Beast*, is summoned to dine with Lord Copper. After being subjected to a summary of Copper's views on everything, he is ordered to send Boot (no Christian name is supplied) to Ishmaelia. Copper is again pilloried as a man of vulgar tastes (see reference to his library and his idea of East Finchley as a country seat), a self-opinionated windbag and a capricious, all-powerful employer. We instantly take to Mr Salter, who does every job he is given as well as he can, but yearns for regular hours and decent anonymity.

Section 4

The day after his dinner with Lord Copper, Salter joins his gloomy managing editor in a horrified study of the shambles that is the day's edition. As they thumb through its pages the name 'Boot' meets their eyes; they instantly believe that 'William Boot, Countryman' is the man Lord Copper wants for some reason to promote, and so the 'mistaken identity' theme of the novel begins. Let it be said that Copper has only himself to blame, for his staff don't want to question his decisions; they are loyal because they fear dismissal: he did mention the Prime Minister (who loves rural novels), and Boot is almost on the staff. His style too seems to be involved or horrible enough to make these simple souls think that it could perhaps be admired.

Textual notes, Sections 1–4

While still a young man It seems that Evelyn Waugh is drawing a parallel, here comparing his own life and output with Boot's, though without being too particular about dates (for example, his first published (as opposed to privately printed) biography *Rossetti* appeared in 1930, when he was 27).

15,000 copies in their first year And obviously more to follow – in fact, he was a 'safe property' for his publisher and agent.

Rimbaud (1854–91); a French poet who turned his back on verse to undertake a variety of work; he travelled much, and spent some time in Abyssinia.

Patagonian Indians Waugh's book *Ninety-two Days* was about travel in British Guiana and Brazil – a far cry from Patagonia in Argentina.

Lady Metroland She first appeared as Mrs Beste-Chetwynde in *Decline and Fall*, Waugh's first novel published in 1928.

Mrs Algernon Stitch She and her husband have been identified in a biographical work, but in view of her very questionable behaviour in one book of the *Sword of Honour* trilogy there is no point in exploring this further.

the Park Either of two parks in London's West End, St James's Park or Green Park.

Nicholas Hawksmoor (1661–1736); better known for his public buildings than his private houses. His style was an 'amalgam of Wren, classical Rome and Gothic', so we are prepared for the opening scene in Mrs Stitch's bedroom.

cul-de-sac Dead-end street.

Saint James's Palace The great brick-built mansion in Pall Mall at the southern end of St James's Street.

a crimson, royally emblazoned dispatch case This indicates that he was a Cabinet minister; it was for his official papers, the sort of article waved about on Budget Day by the Chancellor of the Exchequer.

the Kents The Duke and Duchess of Kent, son and daughter-in-law of George V.

the ideal model for continental caricaturists In fact there were not many statesmen who looked like this.

Labour members loved him It is true that, though opposed to peers officially, they very often enjoyed their company and sought to join their numbers.

an Aztec mask The Indians who inhabited Mexico at the time of Cortez's invasion specialized in frightening representations of the human face.

Miss Holloway The name is associated, here ironically, with the famous London gaol.

a charity ballet A phenomenon of the time was the theatrical performance 'put on' to benefit a good cause.

An elegant young man Waugh may have had in mind Rex Whistler, who decorated the tea-room at the Tate Gallery.

prodigy She was immensely learned and talented for her age.

Virgil The Roman poet (70 BC–19 BC), author of the *Aeneid*.

Brittling Servants were often called by their surnames; this one reminds us of H. G. Wells's novel *Mr Britling sees it through* and we suppose that this means she could cope with everything.

Mrs Beaver A character of this name appears in *A Handful of Dust* – not a very pleasant person.

About the lion's head The whole paragraph shows how Mrs Stitch is a warm capable person who can do a number of things at the same time. Here a captive Mrs Stitch carries on a brisk informed conversation with six tangible people and a telephone voice on a variety of disparate subjects.

Country Life A weekly magazine – glossy, expensive, accurate – read by the upper classes.

Munera Gifts; alternatively, 'duties'.

Bethnal Green Part of the area now known as Tower Hamlets, in the East End of London.

Viola Chasm Note the Christian name, that of a much loved Shakespearian heroine, linked with a surname strongly suggestive of yawning, boring, deep – there are even physical or sexual implications here.

Distressed Area An official name for a district where unemployment was almost total, and apparently incurable.

my Model Madhouse The suggestion is of personal possessiveness, and that there was no limit to Mrs Stitch's relentless do-gooding.

Blakewell Presumably her country house.

Wasters The book's title *Waste of Time* is thus condensed by the slang convention of the time.

Terracotta Brownish red unglazed pottery – one is reminded of Mrs Stitch's clay mask.

hottentot Properly spelt with an initial capital letter. A member of an ethnic group that originally occupied the Cape area of South Africa.

banal Commonplace or trivial. Even for an infant prodigy a new word is of immense interest, and must be employed on every possible occasion.

gymnasium Probably used here in the academic rather than the athletic sense – it probably was a small academy of very intelligent pupils.

two middle-class boys One sometimes feels that Waugh, middle class himself, would have liked to be able to speak like this.

Daimler A large and stately motor car, popular at that time with
  royalty and nobility – and with undertakers.

a midget's funeral hearse A miniature version of her husband's car.

Regency stucco Plaster fronting of the houses built in the Regency
  period (1811–20).

Nash John Nash (1752–1835). His most startling building was the
  Prince Regent's pavilion at Brighton. Nash's buildings were more noted
  for grandiose exteriors than for well-planned interiors, and the stucco
  often concealed rather shoddy brickwork.

Brooks's A famous gentlemen's club on the west side of St James's
  Street.

Arlington Street Probably what is now called Bennet Street, which
  runs between Arlington St and St James's St – which can't be seen from
  Brooks's front door.

Hyde Park Corner to Piccadilly Circus In other words, the entire
  length of Piccadilly.

still as a photograph ... Rich in simile and metaphor, the passage,
  written in 1938, has hints of the Spanish Civil War still in progress
  (barricaded navvies, outposts of some proletarian defence, mining for
  the wires) and a forecast of the greater war still to come.

the bin Abbreviation of 'the loony bin', rather heartless slang for
  'lunatic asylum'.

STRONG LEAGUE NOTE The League of Nations, an earlier version
  of the United Nations, did issue warning notes to nations about to go to
  war, but as the Italian attack on Abyssinia (1935–6) showed, few
  countries took any notice.

Ishmaelia See section 'Background', pp. 9–11.

Foregonners A foregone conclusion, slang like the earlier 'Wasters'.

Lord Copper An appropriate name for the owner of a penny
  newspaper; he has been equated by one biographer with Lord
  Beaverbrook. Note that he is not named for one of the finer metals, and
  that his rival Lord Zinc is named after a compound of various ones. The
  two combined make brass, plenty of which (as cash, or impudence)
  newspaper magnates must have.

Curzon Street North of Piccadilly, close to Shepherd Market.

Megalopolitan Newspaper Corporation From megapolis = great
  city. Lord Copper published many periodicals other than the *Beast*, so
  he needed to incorporate his holdings.

had gotten Transatlantic idiom – and Beaverbrook was Canadian.

riddled through and through i.e. with 'piercing shafts' – a fine
  example of sustained metaphor.

they all played up Naturally, since they all had the same general background.

an uncompromising denunciation If a press baron like Lord Copper took a dislike to a public figure, he would pursue the vendetta on every possible occasion – some of these press lords personally wrote articles on their victims.

He always sleeps ... Boot Well may Lord Copper have been bewildered, for speech cannot show the difference between a common and a proper noun. A boot? To be used as a missile?

Lady Cockpurse A respectable gloss for this word is impossible – it has a touch of Restoration Comedy about it!

Sir Something Hitchcock Again, a bawdy interpretation could be found; but remember that Alfred Hitchcock, the film director, was already quite well known by 1938, the date of the publication of *Scoop*.

Battle of Hastings (1066) The famous battle which signalled the triumph of the Norman Invasion of England.

Daily Brute As Copper and Zinc, barons of base metals, are in competition, it seems only right that their newspapers should fight in the guise of animals.

A microcosm ... of world drama This, of course, was how many people saw the Spanish Civil War: the forces of Germany, Italy and the Soviet Union joined in to gain experience. (A 'microcosm' is a miniature representation.)

Rotarian A member of a Rotary club, one of the many branches of a world-wide society made up of representatives of trades, businesses and professions, organized for the purpose of international service to humanity.

colour-reporters i.e. those who wrote vivid descriptions of events, probably from a distance.

the Poet Laureate John Masefield was Poet Laureate from 1930 – the reference here is to the fact that the *Beast* can attract even the greatest of literary men. It is also a very unpleasant slur on an honourable man.

fifty pounds a week On a temporary contract of course – though it would be a considerable amount for those days.

the Stitch Service But the stitches did not always hold fast.

country seat ... East Finchley The N2 London Postal District was even more built-up than Evelyn Waugh's birthplace in Hampstead.

cabinet pudding A steamed pudding containing dried fruit.

Nazism, Fascism, and Communism Mr Salter already knew, but this did not prevent Lord Copper from giving his views.

Capital of Japan This is, of course, Tokyo.

trick cyclist Here the slang term for 'psychiatrist' is not meant; instead, a popular music-hall or circus act. Note his salary and length of contract compared with that offered for Boot.

Professor Jellaby The name is from Dickens's *Bleak House* – though one could understand every word of Mrs Jellaby's humbug, unfortunately.

Zoo Mercy Slaying A gripping headline – it has everything the readership is reputed to want: animals; pain; killing in kindness; even speculation about the identity of the victim.

Pip and Pop, the Bedtime Pets Inspired by 'Pip, Squeak and Wilfred' from a famous daily of the period; respectively a dog, a penguin and a rabbit.

LUSH PLACES Note the irony of the name – at complete variance with what William is to experience in Ishmaelia. The tradition of having writers on the countryside has not died: Witness the present contributors to, for example, the *Guardian* (none of whom, we hasten to add, is as bad a writer as William).

The Prime Minister is nuts on rural England Stanley Baldwin, who was Prime Minister until 1937, did his best to promote the novels of Mary Webb (1881–1929) which had a rural background (Shropshire). The most famous of her works are *Gone to Earth* and *Precious Bane*.

cider and tinned salmon There speaks metropolitan man – but he may be entirely inaccurate, according to some observers of the time.

Chapter 2

Section 1

In the decaying home of the impoverished Boot family, William receives a telegram summoning him to the headquarters of the *Beast*. His sister in a fit of girlish prankishness has painstakingly altered his last week's copy for *Lush Places*, substituting 'great-crested grebe' for 'badger', thus making nonsense of a carefully-prepared piece of work. William fears the worst, particularly after the letters he has received from puzzled or angry readers. The Boot mansion and its grounds are lovingly described – a fine picture of 'decay in all around' – and the family and their servants are characterized in a style of well-restrained comedy. In Waugh's depiction of country-house society there are echoes of Thomas Love Peacock's

Nightmare Abbey, H. G. Wells's *Bealby* and *Tono-Bungay*, and in a strange reversed way, *Blandings Castle* by P. G. Wodehouse. Christopher Sykes reinforces the last by his belief that Uncle Theodore was inspired by Wodehouse's Galahad Threepwood.

Section 2

Handsomely tipped by Nannie Bloggs, William goes to London; on the train journey he worries about the coming interview with Lord Copper, and determines to defend himself with spirit. He is treated with scorn by a dining-car attendant, and relieved of one of Nannie Bloggs's sovereigns by a shady fellow-traveller. He decides that the town is not for him, and determines to return to Boot Magna by the 10 p.m. train. Now his train arrives at Paddington 'and the atrocious city was all around him'.

Section 3

The Megalopolitan building is described in all its heavy ostentatious vulgarity; William battles his way through to Mr Salter who is described (rather scornfully, one feels) as a townee. He tries to put William at ease by ridiculous references to 'countryside' topics, which are not really understood by either man. Things improve when William shows no liking for what Salter considers the staples of the countryman's diet, and over an expense account dinner the foreign editor puts forward his proposals. The financial rewards are great; the task is made to seem as easy and safe as possible; still William refuses. Then Salter, reluctantly but of necessity, produces his final argument. Lord Copper insists, he says, on his staff working where he tells them to – the alternative is the sack. Sure that William will now accept, he offers him 'a glass of port before we return to the office'.

This section continues to develop the character of William: the born stay-at-home, devoted to the countryside and its familiar life – and Salter: the born urban man, almost terrified of the unknown but guessed-at savagery of rural life. Both men long for security, peace, and the permanent occupation of a harmless, satisfying job. Salter, however, has the advantage, and relentlessly (though uncharacteristically) pursues it. At the restaurant where they dine, another type of newspaper man (Pappenhacker) is pointed out to William; Salter explains the expense-account system, which is to have later repercussions.

Textual notes, Sections 1-3

Change and decay From the hymn *Abide with Me* by H. F. Lyte (1793–1847).

Boot Magna i.e. Great Boot, a suitable name for a village ruled over by the main branch of the family.

Repton Humphrey Repton, a leading English landscape gardener (1752–1818).

malignant disorders that vegetation is heir to A humorous echo of 'the thousand natural shocks that flesh is heir to' (*Hamlet*, III,1, line 63).

cocks Valves controlling the flow of water.

the direct line The branch of the line descended from its founder, not his brothers.

collaterals Descendants of younger sons of founders of the family.

gayest Not in the modern sense of 'homosexual' – it means here that Theodore enjoyed living well, having heterosexual adventures.

Lady Trilby There is a literary association here with George du Maurier's *Trilby*, who was hypnotized by Zvengali; this lady doesn't sound as if she belongs in that category.

the Coming of the Lord Probably a reference to the Bible, (Zachariah 9,14: 'the Lord God shall blow the trumpet'), or even to Julia Ward Howe's celebrated *Battle Hymn of the Republic* with its line, 'Mine eyes have seen the glory of the coming of the Lord.'

Ethelred the Unready (968–1016); King of England.

abeyant i.e. dormant: existent, possibly, but with no one to succeed to the title, even if the estate still continues.

de Butte A Norman-sounding name; perhaps the suggestion is that 'Boot' is the Anglo-Saxon pronunciation, and derives from the older name.

Nannie The two meanings of this word are illustrative of English class-differences: in the upper and middle classes it means their children's nurse; in the working class, a grandmother.

showy doubles Nannie Bloggs would pick an outsider at long odds, and tell the bookmaker that any winnings were to go on a similar horse in the next race. If her forecast were right, she would be well in pocket.

The Bible and the Turf Guide Both books are connected with genealogy, to a greater or lesser extent, but Nannie's researches into horses' breeding and performance were more profitable than Uncle Bernard's.

Chinese Missions i.e. which sent Christian missionaries to China.

Bentinck Note again the choice of name, connected with the members of the distinguished Portland family, who were statesmen.

cadet branch The descendants of the founder's younger brothers.

often blotched with red i.e. with the blood from the butcher's meat.

coupons i.e. containing gift offers and competitions.

at first painfully An indication of William's conscientiousness.

the so-called twentieth century Note how the implied scorn makes nonsense of good English and of what is, often all, a realistic term.

ha-ha A sunken boundary in lieu of a wall or fence, which is not seen until one is upon it.

Cricklewood In the London postal district of NW2, immediately west of Waugh's home suburb of Hampstead, and east of Wembley.

the aged boy Still a junior, though among the Boot pensioners.

elevenses A mid-morning snack – one wonders just how large the servants' midday meal was!

ruminative In the sense of 'requiring prolonged chewing'.

the servants' hall Usually a large room next to the kitchen.

telegrams, in the past Perhaps calling for the repayments of debt, or hush-money, in view of Uncle Theodore's escapades.

doleful, mad eyes Note the exact nature of the description.

three golden sovereigns Long out of currency – part of Nannie's hoard, worth far more than £1 sterling each.

the offside The side farther from the front door.

a chap in Jermyn street This runs parallel to Piccadilly, South side; Mrs Rosa Lewis's hotel, the Cavendish, had an entrance there.

doctrinaire zoology i.e. that which was laid down as policy to be followed.

quids i.e. pounds sterling.

Paddington This suggests that Boot Magna, William's home, was in the West of England.

700–853 Fleet Street A wild exaggeration of the size of the building and of the length of the 'newspaper street' in the City of London, running west from Ludgate Hill to the Strand.

King's Bench Walk In the Temple, south of Fleet Street.

Taunton In Somerset, another indication of the whereabouts of Boot Magna.

tape machines Largely replaced today, but then the news was transmitted from the central agencies and typed automatically on an apparently endless ribbon of white paper.

Byzantine vestibule   Entrance hall in the style of the city of Byzantium (later called Constantinople, now Istanbul), where the classical Greek style was seasoned with rather vulgar Roman ornamentation. The style was wildly extravagant, rather like 'cinema architecture'.

Sassanian   In the style of one of the Persian dynasties (AD 211–651). Again heavily ornamented.

the R.A.C.   Founded in 1897, the original of the Royal Automobile Club. The club referred to is only for people proposed and elected by other members – not for the general run of RAC-badge carriers.

like driven game   Likely to spring into view at any place, at any time.

Caucasian uniform   i.e. in the Russian style: long coats, tightly belted, with flaring skirts, fur caps on heads, knee boots.

Punch-and-Judy accents   Unreal-sounding voices: high-pitched, nasal, with distorted vowels.

chryselephantine effigy   A statue, like that of Olympian Zeus, over-laid with gold and ivory.

polygonal malachite pedestal   A many-sided columnar base made of highly polished green stone – thus the lowly Copper is glorified by precious substances.

concierge   In this case a hall porter, a man of power.

Medals   Waugh is being maliciously ironic – all this is a show to create an impression.

a small vent in his tank   Notice how Waugh once more sustains a metaphor.

We have sixteen peers   Note the irony – they were probably gossip columnists and racing reporters.

hick   Rather a scornful word, an American import for 'yokel', a derogatory word for a countryman.

a large London day-school   Quite likely Hammersmith Latymer (very reputable) or perhaps even St Paul's, considered by Queen Victoria to be a public school.

Welwyn Garden City   Founded in Hertfordshire in 1919, one of a number of towns based on the ideas of Ebenezer Howard (1850–1928). Not a suburb, but an independent town placed in green countryside and having room for industry and cultural activities.

Liverpool Street   The railway station opening off Bishopsgate, in the City of London.

Frinton   A quiet seaside town in Essex, largely populated by the elderly or 'select' young children and nannies.

Flanders In Belgium, scene of some of the great battles of World War I.

its bloody recreations i.e. hunting.

'Mangel-wurzels' A sort of large beetroot cultivated for cattle.

roots A generic term that includes turnips, for example.

churchwarden A long clay pipe – a townsman's idea of a countryman's preference.

Reykjavik The capital of Iceland. The atlas must have been a poor one.

foot and mouth A highly-infectious fever, especially in horned cattle.

Zider The supposed countryman's pronunciation of 'Cider'.

straight rye American whisky, without any dilution.

cheroot A cigar with both ends open.

Garge Salter imagines this version of 'George' is in the country style.

Transportation Sent overseas to labour. Incredibly out-of-date. But remember that William was already in a state of wild alarm.

The mind boggles i.e. wonders, is amazed.

Budapest The capital of Hungary.

Magyar Hungarian.

chafing dish and spirit lamp Tools for the waiter's spectacular act of cooking at the customer's table.

Daily Twopence A quality paper, to judge by the price. It could be Waugh's way of kicking back at *The Times*, which was as mean with its expenses (say some of its reporters) as *The Twopence*.

Most of the staff This does not of course mean that they would refuse to write for a non-Communist paper. Here Waugh is making a sarcastic reference to the left-wing tendencies of many university students.

proletarian A member of the wage-earning or labouring classes.

Asmara In Eritrea, bordering on Abyssinia but far from the fighting.

your life ... insured ... five thousand pounds A larger sum then, but of course insurance is of no personal help to the man who dies.

Fifty pounds Remember that William was struggling along on £150 a year, plus the odd guineas for his articles.

Shanghai ... camels alone Camels would not be found in Shanghai, which is in China.

slap-up Slang for 'excellent'.

Information i.e. which had been received and paid for.

It was a familiar cry ... novices in the past An enjoyable paragraph, full of pathos and owing something perhaps to P. G. Wodehouse's *Psmith, Journalist.*

half-crown i.e. 12½ pence in today's coinage.

Punches The famous humorous weekly (*Punch*) which began
publication in the 1840s.

Serene ... on a day of tempest Note the ironic style, and the use of
contrast to indicate change of mood in response to events.

the austere traditions Again an ironic phrase, particularly in view of
the expense accounts.

Chapter 3

Section 1

Walking up in a London hotel room after retiring late, due to the
hectic round of meetings and introductions at the newspaper offices,
William is roused by the telephone: Salter is calling him to duty.
He parts with much of Lord Copper's money to two hotel servants
– who are not as civil as they might be – and reports to Copper
House.

Section 2

Here, while waiting to see Salter, he is pounced upon by a news
editor, who mistakes him for a new reporter, and despatched to
interview Mrs Stitch, who is sitting in her car at the entrance to
a gentleman's lavatory in Sloane Street. Beautiful, calm and
reasonable, she charms the mob of would-be interviewers into
lifting her car bodily up the stairs, and drives off, composed as
ever, while William is claimed by an anxious Salter, who hurries
him back to see Lord Copper.

Section 3

Lord Copper interviews William in his personal office – as rich
and vulgar as its owner. Lord Copper at once gives William a
lecture on journalism and the leading part played in it by the *Beast*;
he is further told how Lord Copper expects the war to go. It is
emphasized that events must follow the nature of this forecast.
Staggered by his employer's affability, Mr Salter gives William
a respectful but confused address upon the situation in Ishmaelia,

but not before he has told him to rush to buy his equipment. William has been shown (in Section 1) to have been putty in the hands of the hotel staff and, because of his silence in the face of Lord Copper's eloquence, he pleases that gentleman well. Mr Salter gives William an idea of the lightning speed at which a journalist is supposed to move. Will William (ever) be able to rise to this?

Section 4

William kits himself out – or rather, innocent as ever, he lets Miss Barton at the shop do it for him. His expense account has been rather badly dented, and he has enough assorted equipment to delay a whole baggage train, whether in civilization or the wilds.

Section 5

Accompanied by a small moving-van containing his gear, William goes to catch his aeroplane at Croydon. He is happy for the best of reasons – he is going to realize a secret ambition to fly; he barely notices the sparsely-equipped Pappenhacker, who is travelling for the *Twopence*, William is just about to board the regular flight aeroplane when he is approached by the passport officer. What awaits our hero? The section closes with a question mark over William's progress which makes a very useful link with Section 4. The simplicity of William's spirit is shown, and we have our second glimpse of Pappenhacker – much-travelled and preparing for the task ahead. How professional he is, how unlike William in every way.

Textual notes, Sections 1–5

monkey-puzzle A strangely contorted coniferous tree from the Southern hemisphere; the name is self-explanatory.

milking ... cubbing Salter relentlessly continues the rustic line with regard to William – 'cubbing' means hunting young foxes at the beginning of the season.

hired from Cambridge Waugh is here indicating the bias of the

Oxford man who is against anything – here, psychiatry – that is not quite in his view a respectable discipline.

magenta and gamboge Magenta: a brilliant crimson aniline dye discovered shortly after the Battle of Magenta in Italy (1859); gamboge is a gum resin from Cambodian and Siamese trees, which is used as yellow colorant.

women ... could paint their faces Evokes a period, and the rich women of the time.

therapeutic i.e. having curative effects.

High Anglican compromise Here speaks Waugh the uncompromising Catholic convert, censorious of the faith he has left.

a face of ageless evil Page-boys (messengers) were proverbially all knowing and perhaps somewhat depraved.

five shillings i.e. 25 pence in today's coinage, but with far greater buying power then.

two bob Two shillings, i.e. tenpence today.

St Bride's A famous church on the south side of Fleet Street.

dicky An imitation of a starched shirt-front, usually made of 'celluloid', a cellulose compound.

eye shade A visor or green peak.

Sloane Street In Chelsea, London SW1. (At that time, the offices of the Communist Party were at one end, those of the British Union of Fascists at the other, so there was plenty of opportunity for even more sensational happenings than a car in a lavatory!)

expressions ... more careworn Copper's personal staff were even closer to his unpredictable thunder-bolts than was Salter.

prie-dieu Kneeling-desk used for praying – note the implied equation of Lord Copper with God.

purred like warm cats Note the stylistic economy.

depravity of design ... synthetic ivory Nice touches, since there has to be something spurious about anything to do with Copper; 'bell' should be 'bell-push' or 'button'.

satellites Personal attendants grouped around him like the planets around the sun.

Travel Light and Be Prepared There is more than a hint of the Boy Scout about this man.

cleft sticks Letters could be pushed into slots cut in the end – they were standard accessories for African messengers – of a much earlier time!

Remember ... Patriots ... right This is superb, exposing as it does the complete irrelevance with regard to truth that characterizes this newspaper's policy.

We shall expect the first victory A follow-up to the above note; in other words, William must report a 'victory', regardless of actual events.

***That's* Policy** Note that Salter is not Copper's interpreter, merely his loyal servant

White Russians i.e. those who resisted the Russian Revolution of 1917.

Up to a point The use of Salter's phrase, which means 'no' indicates that William is now a fully-fledged *Beast* man.

General Cruttwell The name of Waugh's History tutor at Oxford; he appears here (for the last time in Waugh's work), in an unsympathetic light, as always.

F.R.G.S. Fellow of the Royal Geographical Society.

Spitsbergen An island in the Northern Arctic.

Venezuela One of the two northernmost countries of South America; the other, Colombia, extends a little farther north.

the Pamirs A range of mountains in the USSR.

Cruttwell's leap in Cumberland The northerly parts of our island seem to have been well-patronized by those who leapt – to fame or to death!

Salonika Ceded to Greece after World War I, it is 370 miles south-west of Istanbul.

a sucker i.e. one who can be easily swindled.

a greenhorn A novice, legitimate game for a swindler, but he doesn't have to be easy prey.

a tiffin gun A nonsense – 'a lunch gun'.

chota-pegs Strictly (used nonsensically here), small whiskies.

chota mallet A small mallet. (The 'missionary' was indeed a joker.)

rhinoceros hide whips They make a terrible weal on the victim's body.

a hand-pump i.e. for drawing up water, which will then be sterilized.

astrolabe An instrument, well out of date, for taking altitudes.

humidor This stops cigars from over-drying. (All these purchases reveal just what a sucker William is.)

the Blue Train A fashionable sleeping-car express.

Marseilles Busy French port on the Mediterranean coast.

pantechnicon A van for removing furniture.

Croydon In Surrey. Croydon airport was then much used.

Messageries Maritimes The French mail-ship line.

commercial travellers Nowadays they would be called 'reps'.

the Irish Sweepstake This big draw is still organized today; it was everyone's secret ambition to win the big prize available to the lucky person who 'drew' the Derby winner – with lesser prizes for the other placed horses.

a popish trick Nannie Bloggs has no time for Catholics, particularly if they fail to part with their money.

hacking home Riding back on a spare horse.

fuddled i.e. bemused, a little drunk.

with obeisance With respect, deference – probably including such gestures as bows.

screw i.e. propeller.

Men like gym instructors Because of their muscular build and white overalls.

a seedy soft hat Waugh's dislike of what he considered minor officialdom is here extended to the passport official's clothing.

Chapter 4

Section 1

William, having been stopped at the aerodrome because he has no passport, returns to Copper's headquarters, where the sight of him and his baggage alarms Mr Salter. William is hustled out, and returns to his hotel. He takes a walk in Hyde Park, where he sees (and hears) an Ishmaelian patriot haranguing the crowd.

Section 2

At the Passport Office next day, William is advised to get two visas, one for each Ishmaelian party. First he visits the Patriotic Party's Consulate, where he is treated to a lecture by the Consul (the man he had seen in Hyde Park the previous day), who sells him a visa for £50. He discovers that the Consul is from the West Indies.

Section 3

On going to the rival legation, William finds that the Consul there is from West Africa, a continent's width away from Ishmaelia. After another lecture, even more absurd than the first, he is sold a visa for five shillings (the Consul needs 4/8 to pay a stationer's bill). The consul's temper is as short as his charity is long, for when he sees the first visa he burns the passport.

Section 4

William explains, Mr Salter worries, William gets two passports.

Section 5

William takes off, sharing his plane with a mysterious but obviously important personage.

Section 6

Landing at Le Bourget Aerodrome, William is immediately in trouble with the French Customs, whose officials charge him heavily for his luggage – except for the cleft-sticks. At the Gare de Lyon, he is again beset by officials, and by porters who charge their just but heavy fees for stowing the luggage.

Section 7

William meets again the mysterious stranger, who shared his plane. The man reveals just enough about himself to confuse anyone who has been tempted to judge him by appearances. However, he becomes oddly quiet and politely menacing when William reveals that he is going to Ishmaelia. The section displays a masterly focus on an international 'man of mystery' – still a favourite character of many thriller writers today.

Section 8

William arrives at Marseilles: he sees his dining-companion pass the barrier, but forgets all about him as he has again to cope with his baggage.

Textual notes, Sections 1–8

or someone Salter obviously means himself; like all the staff, he is in terror of Lord Copper.

Archdeacon The clergy are recognized by the Foreign Office as reliable witnesses of passport applications. Note that Archdeacons are fairly senior officers of the Church of England; remember, too, that there are 'at least sixteen peers on the staff'.

a P and O A mail steamer of the Peninsular and Oriental Steam Navigation Company.

Aden In the Gulf of Aden, shortly after it opens out into the Red Sea; opposite the Somali Coast from which Abyssinia can be reached.

Society Beauty A smack at the trivia which make public news.

William turned away He does not want to know about where he is going, but he is no worse than many of those he is going to meet.

Who built the Pyramids Note the rhetorical nonsense of this. They were of course built as tombs and monuments to the Kings of Egypt from the first to the twelfth dynasties.

Maida Vale London W9. A quiet part of Paddington, south-west of St John's Wood. It was becoming a run-down district in the 1930s, so this is a backhander at the small legations.

Yids Slang for 'Jews'.

nigger Again the ignorant servant is made to use a word unacceptable even then.

the clothes were unforgettable He was probably overdressed, rather like Chokey in *Decline and Fall*.

The patriotic cause The Consul repeats the speech he was making the night before in Hyde Park.

There's fifty pounds A hint that he is running a nice little racket.

the first page A pity, as the next section shows.

Antigua A British possession in the Caribbean.

gold swastika The swastika was the emblem of the Nazi party in Germany, just as the hammer and sickle – see previous section – was of the Soviet Union.

a Roman salute Standard fascist practice, a matter for jest at that time.

the Jews of Geneva, subsidised by Russian gold This packs into one sentence the bogeys of Fascism: Jewish finance; Bolshevik Russians; the League of Nations (at Geneva); threat of international intervention.

pure Aryans A manifest absurdity; the mockery, however, is not of the Black but of Hitler, whose abuse of the theme of national purity has brought that phrase everlasting discredit.

Stanley and Livingstone H. M. Stanley (1841–1904) African explorer and journalist; he was sent by his newspaper to discover the whereabouts of Dr Livingstone (1813–1873) African missionary and traveller.

Four and eight to pay i.e. 23 pence in today's coinage.

Sierra Leone On the West African coast – freed slaves were settled there by the British, regardless of the wishes of the original inhabitants. This prepares us for the description of Ishmaelia, on the other side of the continent.

a wad of cotton wool The special plane was for cargo, so had no sound-proofing. Even the passenger planes of that day were noisy.

an empty paper bag i.e. to be sick in, if necessary.

a sand-coloured ulster A heavy overcoat with a cape across the shoulders.

radiating something ... prize Pekingese This may be a patronizing remark, but there is no doubt that Pekingese dogs have a certain dignity.

Le Bourget The airport for Paris.

the rough turf A far cry from the runways of today.

bayed Assailed; surrounded and unable to escape, as a tired stag by hounds.

Tous sont ... usés (Fr); all personal property – all used.

douanier Customs officer.

the jungle scenes of Rousseau Henri Rousseau (1844–1910). He was called 'the douanier' because he was a member of the Paris Municipal Customs Service. He painted scenes of tropical exuberance and extraordinary fantasy, in bright colours and a realistic but primitive manner.

Not since That, too, would have made a fanciful scene for a picture – note the exuberance of the image.

beano A 'bean-feast' – a spree or jollification.

Comment dit-on humidor ... vous savez 'What's a humidor! It's something for keeping cigars in, in the Red Sea – and in this one there's a hospital kit – for cutting off arms and legs, you know; and that's for killing snakes and this is a boat that collapses and these branches (twigs) of mistletoe are for Christmas – for kissing under, you know'. (As William was translating literally from English to French, it adds to the fun if one translates it back literally.)

'Monsieur ...' 'It is not proper to make fun of the Customs' William's explanation would have made even the fanciful Rousseau suspicious.

with sympathy Because the cleft sticks were believed to be connected with sport, and the French – as sports-mad as the English, understood William's (presumed) addiction.

Ils sont ... dépêches ... le Sport 'They're for carrying despatches.' 'Is that a sport?' 'Yes, yes, certainly – Sport.'

Gare de Lyon The station in Paris where one used to board the Paris-Lyons-Marseilles express.

argot Slang.

His head ... Three paragraphs later Waugh repeats the remarks made about wine by M.Leblanc (*Ninety-two days*) who is supposed to be Antonin Besse (1877–1951) with extensive interests in Abyssinia among other places. However, the character in *Scoop* has more in common with Mr Ricketts (see Christopher Sykes's biography of Waugh), and the real persons are obscured by an elaborate embroidery to give an impression of a cosmopolitan financial adventurer.

cabochon Polished, but not cut into shapes or facets.

pearls and platinum The chain carrying his watch at one end and some other accessory at the other.

Turkish The suggestion is of a man of wide international background.

Levantine Of the islands and mainlands of the Eastern Mediterranean.

Eurasian Any combination of European or Asian blood strains. (The word is not so much used today as it was at the time of *Scoop*.)

Latin Of the European peoples who speak languages derived from Latin, though they are not necessarily of Roman descent.

Teuton The German-speaking peoples.

The moment It was a common belief that all people of ambiguous nationality wanted to be taken for Englishmen.

Bordeaux Great French seaport, commercial and industrial city and wine centre.

Château-Mouton-Rothschild A magnificent claret named after a real place. Note how the whole paragraph is in the manner of a 'wine-snob' report.

rococo snuff-box Highly ornamented.

a coroneted crêpe-de-Chine Titled as well as monied, he can afford expensive silk handkerchiefs.

coupé A private compartment at the front of a railway carriage.

a fellow Englishman Again the claim to national kinship.

Côte d'Azur On the French Mediterranean coast.

We march with The district we hunt over.

Antibes An exclusive (at that time) seaside resort on the French Mediterranean coast.

pre-Hitler German poetry Presumably a reference to the fact that the poet may have been a German Jew, whose work would be banned in Hitler's time (i.e. 1933 onwards).

consommé to bombe Clear soup to ice-cream pudding.

cachets Tablets.

conducteur The head sleeping-car attendant.

A very courageous man One never ceases to be amazed by this man; he now says he served in the British Army as an Officer, and he has one of his soldiers as a servant – like Bulldog Drummond or Richard Hannay.

V.C. Victoria Cross.

Chapter 5

Section 1

William boards the old-fashioned mail steamer and meets two stock characters of adventure novel and film: the French colonial administrator, deeply suspicious of the perfidious English, but doting on his family; the Captain who makes his ship his home, and does a little smuggling as a sideline. William is then joined by the extraordinary Corker, who talks rapidly and endlessly and is very knowing about the journalistic trade – though he has only been a minor reporter – and puts over an 'old-stager' act. He gives William (and the reader) brief character sketches of some of the journalists already in Ishmaelia.

Section 2

Having rashly eaten tainted fish, Corker retires to his cabin, where William seeks him in order to discover the meaning of a wireless message. Corker is strangely reticent and unhelpful.

Section 3

While bargaining for curios in Aden, Corker receives a radiogram which tells him that his agency is now engaged by the *Beast*. He at once becomes friendly again, and translates William's message. William again meets the mysterious stranger; this time he adds to the mystery by carrying a Costa Rican passport.

Section 4

Aden. Corker is busy amassing more curios, trying to interview important people, and giving William a lesson in cable-ese.

In London, John Boot meets Mrs Stitch at a ball. She is surprised to see him, and can't understand why her plan has miscarried, though she is non-committal in her remarks.

Textual notes, Sections 1–5

Francmaçon (Fr); Freemason

Gulf of Suez Runs from the south end of the Suez Canal into the Red Sea.

long chairs i.e. reclining-chairs, giving some air and rest to passengers in intense heat.

heraldic Heavily ornamented with coats-of-arms.

'Lunce pliss' Lunch, please.

apocalyptic Concerning a great revelation (as in the Bible): of course the meaning here is heavily ironic: he is going through the motions of announcing lunch – the last thing most of the passengers want!

the functionary a rather scornful word for 'civil servant'.

If it were rich A general but prejudiced view of 'British Imperialism'.

Ah, well, to the journalist Double meaning; the journalist makes money from practising his trade in any country he goes to (and padding his expense account) and he is inclined to see wealth where very little exists.

cummerbund A broad sash wrapped round the waist.

blatant domesticity All-too-apparent family life.

contraband i.e. smuggled goods.

War is all commerce True, at least to some extent: the point of view was then fashionable, but lost much force in 1939.

Peut-être (Fr); perhaps.

Gallic scepticism As the functionary demonstrated, the French made a point of doubting, even scorning, the viewpoints of others. (Throughout the book Waugh makes fun of foreigners.)

charger i.e. large flat dish.

barbed fly An artificial fly, fastened to a hook, resting on the surface to lure the trout.

chaste silver dishes Like the rest of the passage, contrasting with William's present surroundings – true metal, simple design, as opposed to elaborate imitation.

distant Canaan There are many Biblical references to Canaan; it is the land of promise – heaven – here the rich country from which William has been exiled.

deserted Eden i.e. lost by Adam and Eve when they sinned. William of course means England.

'Il faut ... vivre ... comme viande' 'One must eat – one must stay alive. What sort of meat is there?'

miasmically In this sense, like a floating mist.

djinn A spirit, lower than the angels, that can take human form. Its terrible destiny seems to be the performance of any errand devised by the human who can control it.

paterfamilias The father of a family.

a whopper i.e. a very large one (lady).

the Continental Figure Huge bosom, massy buttocks, thick in-between.

Hi, you, Alphonse ... bitter Hi, Alphonse, do you understand pint of bitter?

comme ça Like this.

Beaucoup A lot (of), very much.

toute-de-suite Immediately.

U.N. Universal News.

mauvais poisson ... vite le whisky Bad fish – strong smell – take it – and bring whisky quickly.

matey Friendly

la belle France Beautiful France.

Ostend The Belgian port and seaside resort.

Edward VIII Edward VIII had just abdicated after a very short reign; this proves that the whisky was not very old.

Saigon In what was then French Indo-China, and is now Vietnam: the whisky was of course not genuine Scotch.

Regency buck i.e. a man of fashion of the Regency period when the Prince of Wales (later George IV) was made Regent during George III's illness – early 19th century.

quizzing glass A sort of monocle on a short wand.

East Sheen A suburb of South London, near Richmond.

cut up very nasty i.e. turned unpleasant.

your traps i.e. your luggage.

news agency Reuter's was the best known. They employed their own reporting staff and supplied news to journals.

specials i.e. special reporters, men capable of writing 'features'.

curios i.e. having a curiosity value; mementoes, hardly antiques.

Colour is just a lot of bull's-eyes Background information ('local colour') is of no importance.

Corker recounted ... He is represented as confirming all the superstitions of the would-be knowing reader.

a rise of screw An increase of salary.

scooped the world i.e. was the first to report.

the *Lusitania* A passenger liner, carrying many Americans, which was sunk by a German submarine in 1915, and is thought to have been instrumental therefore in the American decision to aid the Allies.

Hitchcock, the English Jakes He is reminiscent of the American newspaper proprietor whose tendentious reporting is said to have caused the start of the Spanish/American war.

the Messina earthquake A horrifying natural disaster in Sicily in 1908. It shows that Hitchcock had been around for a long time.

Corker himself His experience with the knight's widow is rather like William's with Mrs Stitch in the public convenience.

syndicated Published simultaneously in all the newspapers which chose to pay for his work.

a thousand dollars At that time worth £200.

Balkan Of Bulgaria, Roumania, Yugoslavia, Albania, for example.

There's the power of the press for you A magnificent piece of irony that underlines the central satirical emphasis of the book.

nettle-rash So called because its blisters resemble nettle-stings. Corker was suffering from food-poisoning or, at least, an allergic reaction to the fish.

Vichy water A bottled mineral-water, unflavoured, much used by those who mistrust a local water supply.

OPPOSITION ... BEAST Translated in detail on the next page (p.69) of the novel.

distinctly unmatey Noticeably unfriendly.

Steamer Point That part of Aden where the ships tied up and the night life was to be found (see *When the Going was Good*).

companion ladder Here a stairway rigged to the side of the ship with a platform at the foot from which boats may be boarded.

clinker A mass of slag or lava – Aden was built upon an extinct volcano.

synthetic ivory Made from a compound called bakelite; just the sort of thing Corker would be deceived by.

francs to rupees i.e. French currency and the Indian currency that was also used in British East Africa. At that time the rupee was worth two shillings and sixpence (12½ pence in today's coinage.)

sat in judgment i.e. checked that the passports were correct.

hair-wash A lotion for the hair, rather more delicate than hair oil.

Warmth Another example of the evasive nature of his answers.

Costa-Rican So the English traveller had the passport of a Central-American Republic.

pansy The mysterious traveller was not a homosexual, but Corker believes that anyone so jewelled and scented could not be anything else.

stuffed mermaid 'A seedy ... sea-animal, unmistakably male' kept in a hotel in Aden and displayed for money.

the wells of Solomon Water tanks constructed it is said, at the orders of the celebrated Queen of Sheba.

Benares trays Indian brasswork (usually made in Birmingham).

Tutankhamen's sarcophagus The coffin of the Egyptian pharaoh of the 18th dynasty; died aged 18 in c.1340 BC. There have recently been world-wide exhibitions of the treasures (mainly of gold) found in his tomb at Thebes by Lord Carnarvon and Howard Carter in 1922.

emporium Pompous name for a shop.

the Resident The British official in charge of the Protectorate.

sloop A smallish warship – the name had been recently reintroduced in the Royal Navy.

the focal point Corker's way of hitting back at the uncooperative Resident and Captain.

UNWARWISE i.e. unprepared.

the little Italian port The coastal terminus of the train to Abyssinia is Djibuti in what was then French Somaliland. Making the town Italian seems to be designed to make us think that Ishmaelia is not Abyssinia.

the Duchess of Stayle Pun on 'stale' perhaps, and a 'refined' would-be-superior pronunciation of 'style'.

Elderly princesses ... pools of deportment A fine metaphor – they would be surrounded by groups of courtiers and hangers-on.

loped Superb choice of word, with its animal suggestions.

foie-gras A pâté made from goose-livers: very expensive.

bog-oak from Tipperary Ancient wood, preserved in Irish peat.

Book 2 Stones £20

Chapter 1

Section 1

This opens with an account of the history of Ishmaelia, the country which is to occupy the foreground of the action. There follows a description of the ruling family, perpetuated by a series of 'Jackson Ngomas' (General Elections), preceded in each case by a banquet.

Ishmaelia is a member of the League of Nations; but the more important focus is on the Jackson domestic row, which leads to the establishment of two opposing parties and threatens to undermine the regime. In the chief cities of Europe it is believed that there will be a war in Ishmaelia.

Section 2

A description of the Hotel Liberty, Jacksonburg, and of Mrs Earl Russell Jackson and her clientele. First, Wenlock Jakes and *Under The Ermine*; then the four furious Frenchmen, the group of correspondents and Erik Olafsen; Pappenhacker, the representative of *The Twopence*; finally, Sir Jocelyn Hitchcock, asleep in the annexe.

Section 3

The journey to Jacksonburg of William and Corker, the camera crew and their companions, is described. On the train there is also a mysterious Swiss 'ticket collector' who is treated with much deference. The luggage van is detached from the rest of the train; Corker loses his curios. He and William meet the other journalists in Jacksonburg.

Section 4

Corker, Pigge and William in a brief discussion about the situation in Ishmaelia.

Section 5

Jakes interrogating his man Paleologue about the whereabouts of Hitchcock and the other journalists.

Section 6

Shumble has got some kind of a scoop, but refuses to divulge it, though he is questioned by his fellow journalists and by Erik Olafsen.

Section 7

Describing the frustrations of the journalists as they try to get hold of 'boys' to take messages for them.

Section 8

Paleologue agrees to provide servants for the journalists; he takes his own cut of the payments made to them.

Section 9

Conversation between Corker and William; Corker tries to question Mrs Earl Russell Jackson about affairs in Jacksonburg; William and Corker then go off to see Erik Olafsen; Shumble keeps his news to himself.

Section 10

William and Corker go to the Press Bureau, but the Director is away. William meets an old school friend of his, 'Moke', who turns out to be the Vice-Consul; 'Moke' invites 'Beastly' (William) to dinner than evening.

Section 11

Shumble's world scoop re the Red agent in Ishmaelia is published. Everyone goes off to look for Russians. Benito denies the story, and William cables his newspaper that it is 'all rot'.

Section 12

William dines with Jack 'Moke' Bannister, who explains the Ishmaelite situation to him – including the nonsense of its map. For instance, there is no such place as Laku; it is the Ishmaelite word for 'I don't know'. He tells William of the arrival of the Russian Jew in Jacksonburg. On his return to the hotel, William wakes Corker and tells him what he has learned at dinner. Corker replies that William's story is 'dead' – killed by the previous denial of Shumble's scoop.

Section 13

Sir Jocelyn Hitchcock pins his flag on the map over the city of Laku.

Textual Notes, Sections 1–13

Ishmaelia Presumably called after Abraham's second wife Hagar; Ishmael was cast out to roam with her in the wilderness (Genesis, Chapters 16 and 21). Nomadic Arabs sometimes claim to be his descendants. In some ways this fictional country resembles Abyssinia, for example in its remote capital connected to the coast by an erratic railway, its 'squireens' and the landless men who infest its capital. It too is under the wing of the League of Nations, and is the home of many outcast foreigners. Whatever the source of his inspiration, Waugh has painted a fascinating picture of a complex, seedy society which had (and has) its equivalents in other parts of the world.

Dark Continent A 19th-century phrase; Africa was 'dark' for more reasons than one, but mainly because so little was known of its interior.

Berlin and Geneva Berlin the capital of Germany, Geneva the Swiss home of the League of Nations.

None returned ... eaten Waugh's interest in cannibalism was earlier shown in *Black Mischief*.

in the nineties ... themselves The 1890s, but here Waugh is summing up in two sentences the principles of the nations involved in what was known as 'the grab for Africa'.

bicameral Having an upper and lower chamber of representatives in Parliament.

secular education i.e. not run by any church.

habeas corpus The right of a prisoner to be brought before a judge so that his condition can be examined and his continuing existence guaranteed.

joint stock banking Its initial capital was provided by the sale of shares, which made the bank answerable to a number of people, not just one financier.

Samuel Smiles Jackson Samuel Smiles was a 19th-century author, famous for his *Self-Help* (1859). He was also the biographer of, among others, poor boys who made good: a very apt choice of name for a member of the Jackson family.

a Mr Rathbone Jackson The names that follow are a reflection of Waugh's satirical regard for the institutions and entertainment of the time: Basil Rathbone was a cinema actor, still famous for his portrayal of Sherlock Holmes; Pankhurst was named after the formidable leader of the suffragettes; Garnett, the name of a literary family; Mander (Miles) another film actor who played villain's parts; Huxley (notice he had an uncle and brothers) is named after the famous English family that included a number of scientists and a novelist, all influential.

quinquennial Every five years.

General Gollancz Jackson Named after the left-wing publisher, Victor Gollancz, rather than the London University Professor, Sir Israel Gollancz.

Mule Taxgathering ... Artillery Death Duties Corps This makes it clear that they were intended for internal duties, not for external aggression

silver coinage In many parts of East Africa the old Maria Theresa dollars (which were still being minted in Austria) were the favourite currency.

cover in kind: Crops, animals and so on – a picture of intense confusion at the bank is conjured up.

Under the liberal ... prospered ... incredulously heard Note the irony, with its concise account of a confused state of affairs.

safari Organized expedition for the shooting of game.

if they returned at all An ominous qualification, with hints of violent death and cannibalism.

Assistant Director of Public Morals The prostitutes and other caterers for vice would have paid their commissions to his departmental chief.

a manifesto ... composed himself A hint here of outside Fascist influence.

The White Shirt Movement A satire against the Black Shirt Movement of Mussolini, the Italian Fascists.

his thesis It was repeated to William in London, and is familiar to European readers; one has only to substitute 'Jewish' for 'Negro' throughout to realize the Fascist source of these utterances.

Bolshevism i.e. Communism, as exemplified by Russia.

Armenian One of a Middle Eastern ethnic group, noted for their trading ability (though this one slipped up).

Harlem ... Liberia Harlem, the New York Black quarter; Bloomsbury, a gathering place for intellectuals, usually prosperous and left-wing in tone; Liberia, in Africa, here mentioned as the country chosen for the reception of freed American slaves (and other non-African negroes).

sacerdotalism A doctrine which implies that priests have a special voice in the ruling of the nation.

chapels and universities A hint that the Nonconformist Christianity and higher education favoured socialism.

a little worker's daughter in Bedford square Although not in its hey-day, Bedford Square, Bloomsbury (home of Virginia Woolf) did not have many 'workers' – unless they were domestic servants. The 'three unused penny' stamps were obviously sent by an intellectual rather than 'a little worker's daughter'.

Hotel Liberty A predictable name, just as Jacksonburg was.

Mrs Earl Russell Jackson Named after Bertrand Russell (1872–1970), celebrated philosopher, mathematician and eccentric.

commercial cafés and domino saloons At that time London too had its Mecca cafés, where city clerks drank coffee and the clatter of dominoes on marble table-tops filled the air.

austere trade Strict self-discipline drove them to work.

King Edward's abdication Edward VIII (later Duke of Windsor, who married Mrs Simpson) abdicated in 1936.

dining at the Savoy grill The Savoy Grill (in the Savoy Hotel, in the Strand) is one of London's most famous restaurants, and has always been much favoured by American visitors.

News Chronicle This was an amalgamation of two earlier newspapers, the *Daily News* and the *Morning Chronicle* – but it wasn't the kind of paper to have had much access to State secrets.

John Nought Assurance companies have vast numbers of 'noughts' in their accredited capital.

Credential An obvious corruption of 'Prudential', with an added sense of respectability – if anything could be more respectable than the Prudential insurance company.

20,000 dollars Then £4,000, on account of royalties.

four furious Frenchmen Here the parody of the French foreign correspondent begins.

Shumble, Whelper, Pigge Each name is an insult – and an obvious one too.

The Swede was ... of high standing Vice-consuls were sometimes business or professional men who were only part-time representatives of their countries' diplomatic services.

Tea, Bible and Chemist shop A useful portmanteau title – and institution.

four no hearts ... no hearts What makes this impossible call worth a note is Olafsen's simple logic.

College He had won a scholarship, and boarded with others like himself.

Winchester The famous public school founded in 1387 by William of Wykeham.

Latin alcaics Verses in the metre of an early classic poet Alcaeus (c. 600 BC).

derive Greek names Many modern scientific names are built up from Greek roots.

turnover Useful as reserve reporting if nothing was happening.

wildly deceptive map It is, after all, to be Hitchcock's downfall.

And the granite sky wept A telling metaphor, embodying images of harshness, sombreness, despair, yet perhaps not symbolic.

Spahi French North African native cavalry, whose voluminous cloaks were a spectacular part of their uniform.

Jakes' jackal The word 'jackal' is used to describe a person who does preparatory drudgery for someone else – as the jackal was believed to hunt the lion's prey for him.

beaver Slang name for a 'beard'.

collect facilities i.e. to receive and send messages.

urgenting Telegraphese for 'sending urgent news'.

ambassador We see later that he was one, in a way.

soldiers of fortune Mercenary soldiers, prepared to fight for pay, often as commanders of untrained troops.

mystery men i.e. agents of foreign powers, fortune-hunters.

volunteers In the context of 1938 (the novel's publication date) this meant regular troops of armies of great powers, thinly disguised as ardent supporters of one side or the other. In Spain, for example, Franco was supported by German and Italian Army and Air Force 'volunteers'; the Government was supported by Soviet Russia.

Paleologue He bears the name of a dynasty of Emperors of Byzantium.

dragoman Guide to the embassy's visitors; messenger.

provide amusement i.e. arranged for them to have girls.

exiguous Scanty, small.

Kingsley Wood In fact one of the least colourful of Cabinet Ministers – a short, cherubic Postmaster-General.

rummy Odd.

draconic, arbitrary, venal It makes rigid regulations; its decisions suit itself; it allows no dispute; it can be bribed.

Adventist Mission We normally think of Seventh Day Adventists: whatever this sect, it was Nonconformist, possibly extreme, and well-enough supported financially to have a University in Alabama.

a dollar a week Probably one of the Maria Theresa dollars mentioned in the note on silver p.56.

tight i.e. drunk.

INTERNATIONAL GENDARMERIE An armed police force from a variety of members of the League of Nations – rather like today's United Nations peacekeeping force.

sissy i.e. effeminate, not masculine.

sit-upon i.e. bottom.

Staunchly anti-interventionist When the novel was written, the idea of intervention was a popular one. It was being considered as a solution to the Spanish Civil War.

Doyen Senior member.

Café de la Bourse 'The Stock Exchange café'.

Carnegie Library One of a chain founded by the American millionaire philanthropist Andrew Carnegie (1835–1919).

Ciné-Parlant Talking picture cinema – a bit behind the times, since silent films were a relic of the past, and had been so for at least eight years.

Armenian liquor An indication of the variety of nationalities involved in small trading here.

Goanese tailoring Done by the people of Goa (then a Portuguese possession) in India who had a considerable reputation as reliable workers in East Africa.

The American Welfare Centre Commonly found in large cities, also in remote areas.

Popotakis's Ping-Pong parlour Fine example of almost nonsensical alliteration, the athletic man's alternative to the domino saloons.

rock-salt ... paraffin The order of this list is not haphazard, but represents the priorities of isolated savage people.

Benito Benito Mussolini (1883–1945), 'Il Duce', was the Fascist leader of Italy, determined to reassert Rome's former glory, and intent on conquest in Africa. He was both dangerous and ridiculous.

hawk i.e. sell.

Badly left i.e. you've missed a good news story.

Echo splashing The *Echo* has the story of a Soviet spy all over its front page.

Kindly investigate ... cable deferred rate Note the politeness and the proverbial economy of *The Twopence* (of course *The Times* is meant by Waugh).

or boil i.e. suffer (because we haven't discovered anything).

dementi A diplomatic way of saying that this story is a lie and must be contradicted.

Legation compound The grounds in which the residence of a diplomatic mission stands.

first secretary Second in command of the mission.

Laku The story touched off much useless activity among the journalists, because Hitchcock believed 'the official, wildly deceptive map' to be accurate, though Benito of course knew it to be false.

F.O. Foreign Office.

Wish we knew ... Seven important paragraphs – the facts are worth remembering.

bogus Fake.

standoffish Distant.

jibbing i.e. refusing to commit itself.

A Jew straight from Moscow A standard bogey of the time of sensationalist newspapers, thriller-writers etc.

H.M.G's book His Majesty's Government's best interests.

a tip-off i.e. an indication, a clue, a lead.

That story's dead Jakes had seen to that. The paragraph shows Corker's view of events. The press corps had denied the story and could not be shown to be wrong, even though William's report showed there was some truth in it.

the spot marked This shows that he is going to invent a story, as Jakes did in the Balkans. Hitchcock does not intend to go to Laku, but proposes to write up events that he believes are likely to happen (as he had done about the Messina earthquake). In fact, he intends to scoop Jakes more than any other reporter, but Jakes has been on the spot (even though it is the wrong one) and Hitchcock is going to write about a non-existent place.

Chapter 2

Section 1

While the other journalists get on with their various tasks, William and Corker set out for the station to look for their lost luggage; the taxi driver takes them instead to Olafsen's shop. Olafsen talks of 'my friends' Shumble, Whelper and Pigge. There is an interruption when a white girl comes in, buys something, and goes out again. Olafsen says she is a married German lady, whose husband has gone away. He adds that twenty more journalists are to arrive that evening.

Section 2

William and Corker are disgusted by the food they have to put up with. They receive cables from their respective papers.

Section 3

Everyone goes to meet the evening train, which, however, does not bring the expected distinguished visitor; but William's and Corker's lost luggage arrives. About fifty journalists and photographers disembark, many of whom sleep in William's room; next day, on the advice of Moke Bannister, William moves.

Section 4

William's move is to the Pension Dressler. Frau Dressler, her rooms and her animals are described, as well as the peasants who surround her establishment. William is to have the best room, which turns out to belong to the German woman they had seen at Olafsen's. William talks to her and allows her to leave a heavy bag (full of stones) in his room. She is rather amused by his remarks about the cleft sticks; together they assemble the canoe but are interrupted in this romantic episode by Corker. He brings news that Hitchcock has gone to Laku to scoop the world; there is to be a meeting of the foreign press association that evening to discuss matters. The

German girl sells her husband's stone specimens to William for £20.

Section 5

The meeting of the Foreign Press Association, an acrimonious one, is described, with stray snatches of multilingual dialogue forming the main content of the meeting. Dr Benito arrives to address the meeting, and says that the journalists may travel to the interior, provided they obtain formal passes. William of course knows that there is no such place as Laku.

Section 6

William is to stay in Jacksonburg; he plays ping-pong with Kätchen.

Section 7

The chaos following the departure of the journalists is described. William refuses to go to Laku, despite the insistence of Dr Benito.

Section 8

William sees off the expedition to the Interior [or Lakuwards, as the cablers would prefer it]. But the journalists don't get beyond the barricades of the town on this first venture, and have to be freed by Dr Benito to continue their journey the next morning.

Textual notes, Sections 1–8

The Archbishop of Canterbury There in essence we have Jakes – his greatness and his littleness. His publishers will doubtless be sued for libel for this kind of sensationalism.

Imperial Chemicals Note that this still flourishes today. One of its founders was Jewish, so we see Waugh making fun of two institutions he did not care for – 'Jewish finance' and the Church of England.

a blinded and shackled Samson But the big Swede will later burst his metaphorical bonds and bring down the heathen temple (Chapter 5, p.173).

gum boots Wellington boots.

the Garbo Greta Garbo, the Swedish actress, was born in 1905, still alive in 1979 – a beautiful woman and a first-class actress, who had a great influence on film acting.

pension Boarding house.

Frau Dressler Waugh was clearly interested in, and knowledgeable about, the cinema. He is perhaps thinking here of Marie Dressler (1869–1934) a large woman with an ugly but compelling face who specialized in playing bossy but not insensitive women. In *A Biographical Dictionary of the Cinema* David Thompson says she was 'as close to Mother Courage as Hollywood could run'.

confrères i.e. brother journalists.

the absence of Hitchcock Interesting figure of speech: 'presence' more often lies heavily, but Hitchcock continually posed the threat of a scoop, whether absent or present.

PRESUME YOUR STEPTAKING ... GENERAL UPBREAK We presume that you are taking steps to ensure uninterrupted transmission of news in the event of a general breakdown of posts, cables etc.

Derby hat The American name for a bowler.

daguerrotype An early type of photograph (named after photographic pioneer Louis Daguerre, 1789–1851), the image being formed on a sensitized silver plate treated with mercury vapour.

a Victorian worthy There *was* a Victorian atmosphere about the Jackson family. Waugh makes use of the photographic black-and-white metaphor two or three times in the book.

chaff and gin They made fun of each other and bought each other drinks.

It's ideological It's all in the mind.

Bad policy i.e. because William won't then be able to keep an eye on his fellow journalists.

guests – baboons ... milch goat A mixed bag, guests and animals, but the really malevolent presence was the goat. It, like Frau Dressler, had complete control in its own sphere of influence.

Indian hemp The drug which has a score of names – hashish, for example, and a number of nicknames.

his brief waking hours The greatest asset for an African nightwatchman was the ability to sleep his night away.

Tanganyika A large territory, under German control until 1918, south of Kenya and Uganda.

patois dialect.

like a cork ... popgun There is a pleasant touch of the ridiculous about this simile.

gander Geese are proverbially good sentries.

How about trying mistletoe? Corker senses that William is already much taken with the girl.

Bergner Elizabeth Bergner (b. 1898) a German actress who did more stage than film work; she came to England in the early '30s and made her home here. Her best-known film was *Escape Me Never*. Bergner had a 'gamine' style, hence Corker's 'whimsical'.

Kätchen This German diminutive of a girl's name also means 'kitten' – as indeed she was: playful, easily hurt, and tough.

Ten English Pounds Here one sees Kätchen's toughness; she already knows that she can do what she likes with William, and makes her first attempts at exploitation, deploying her 'husband' as a useful protection against any advances by William.

Note that this section resembles the 'change and decay' description of Boot Magna in Book 1. There are many parallels between the Pension Dressler, even down to the servant population, though the Pension has rather different animals!

Order ... motion as amended reads The next $2\frac{1}{2}$ pages (117–19) are a picture of polyglot disorder, portraying the journalists as a group of temperamental opera stars (almost a folk-image of the period).

je vous en prie I beg you.

Paris-soir A Parisian evening paper.

Havas French news agency.

On traite ... légèreté indésirable This is the literal translation of the English words above: 'this whole question ... undesirable levity.'

If you pliss Conventional guying of stage German accent. (It is interesting to note that Kätchen's speech is not travestied in this way.)

Italiano ... piacere Italian ... please.

tutte domanda con levita spiacevole See 'On traite' above.

a scab Trade unionist word for one who refuses to strike.

pipe down Stop talking, be quiet.

Notre condition professionelle ... égale et libre The French translation of the sentence above '... our professional status ... fair and free competition'.

Nostra condizione professionale Italian version of 'our professional status'.

soot-black in face ... brilliantly white Almost a black-and-white minstrel parody description.

I have a communication to make A fine piece of Civil Service jargon. 'You are under the President's control. He has made no exceptions for anybody.'. Now comes the punch. 'Travel to the interior is dangerous – but you can go.' The prosaic words hide a deep hope that they will get lost – metaphorically and literally.

blackamoor Archaic derogatory term for a Black.

a cable Worth translating in parts; it is a gem: Don't go to Laku. Remain and keep in touch with Red sympathizers. We have received no news from you. It is most essential that you should send us accurate daily reports. Remember the cable rates – one and six [one shilling and sixpence: $7\frac{1}{2}$p in today's coinage] a word.

ravan-boys (Should be 'caravan-'.)

seminarists The most likely of the definitions is 'priests in training' – in this case Ishmaelites.

benzine A petroleum product, used for cooking stoves and lamps.

exodus i.e. when everyone left.

Parsee A follower of the Zoroastrian creed, descended from Persians who fled to India in 7th–8th centuries to escape Muslim persecution.

Banja Probably Bania – an Indian merchant.

cornered All supplies bought by one person who could thus make a huge sales profit.

sunproof shirts Sometimes called bush-jackets, of stout material supposed to ward off the dangerous rays of the sun.

Newmarket boots Leather feet, canvas tops reaching to the knee, waterproof and more comfortable than gum-boots.

Chapter 3

Section 1

Kätchen's appearance greatly improved, and William falls in love with her in a predictable, romantic way.

Section 2

Sir Jocelyn Hitchcock considers everything is over, and is ordered to proceed to Lucerne. He meets Erik Olafsen, who accompanies him to Popotakis's; there they meet William. Erik reveals that, when very young, he killed his grandfather with a chopper after drinking too much absinthe. Hitchcock gives William the benefit of his experience, and when he has gone William is left as the only special correspondent in Jacksonburg.

Section 3

William and Kätchen together, having a slight tiff that leaves William in a state of 'light melancholy'.

Section 4

Frau Dressler speaks to Kätchen in the Pension dining-room; afterwards Kätchen begins to cry. William comforts her and asks her if she is really married. She reveals that she isn't, and leaves him alone at the breakfast table.

Section 5

Corker and Pigge, twelve miles out of town, complaining about their black servants. They are bogged down in mud, miles from anywhere.

Section 6

William drives out to the Consulate to see Bannister. The latter hints that William should watch Dr Benito, and invites him to bring Kätchen to dinner 'one evening'. Then he tells William that in London there are rumours that he (William) has been murdered.

Section 7

Copper House, with Salter and his companions bemoaning William's lack of activity in Ishmaelia.

Section 8

Back with William and Kätchen; William is receiving unpleasant cables from the *Beast*. Kätchen squeezes some money out of William for 'expenses', and teases him somewhat, though she spends the night with him.

Textual notes, Sections 1–8

vanity case Clearly described here, but not much in use today.

the bucolic jaunts i.e. 'tumbling in the hay' was as strange to William as the questionable pleasures of expensive brothels.

land-bound A telling metaphor – his energies had been centred on his land and home.

A lush place An echo, a reference back to the column that had so delighted him, had brought him to the squalor of Ishmaelia, and was now bringing him fresh delights.

eau de quinine A scalp tonic.

PROCEED LUCERNE One would have thought Geneva, home of the League of Nations, but that organization did change its meeting place from time to time. Non-intervention was the theory of not giving economic aid to either side in a war.

French two-step i.e. dance music blared.

baccarat A game of cards played between a 'banker' and punters for money.

polyglot Speaking many languages.

rendezvous Meeting place.

grenadine A French cordial made from the fruit of the granadilla, a S. American and Caribbean variety of passion flower.

There were parrots He had been at the absinthe, so perhaps it had given him delusions, or perhaps he was just trying to provide some background to Laku, which he had of course not visited.

Exactly ... interview ... the place There had been, however, no interview. This paragraph provides an interesting slant on reporting abroad. It was expensive, and results were expected even if they had to be invented. Shumble's effort was based on a false rumour, but Hitchcock's is infinitely worse.

Kätchen was sitting ... began to cry There was no pretence here, for Frau Dressler had been giving her a bad time.

Pernod A brand name for a milder form of absinthe.

metalled strip The strip of hard road surface for lorries etc, with earth tracks for pedestrians and animals on each side.

opening some tins A spicy, horrible broth. The benzine flavour came from the cooking stove.

crapulous i.e. drunken.

Paleologue's been trying Finding little girl friends for lonely bachelors was one of his specialities.

F.O. Foreign Office.

I have to denounce ... weather is improving He knew quite well that he was making a wonderful blaze of mixed metaphors, and his perfectly straightforward last sentence is all the more heartfelt.

Then you will pay me With even less practice than William, Kätchen has mastered the expense-account system.

vermouth A liqueur consisting of white wine flavoured with wormwood and other herbs: intended to be used as an appetizer.

The three-legged dog awoke ... protest A fine, poetic sentence, which also symbolizes the human misery and discomfort in that place.

Chapter 4

Section 1

William awakes next day, and the rains are over; but his 'boy' has gone.

Section 2

Olafsen leaves because there is 'plague down the line', and Kätchen returns with her shopping. She also reveals that the President has been locked up. In a laconic cable, William sends the news of this together with the account of Benito and the Russian Jew to the *Beast*. William in turn receives a cable sacking him.

Section 3

Corker and Pigge still mudbound twelve miles from town.

Section 4

A party at the British Legation, to which William goes alone. There he meets Bannister, who introduces him to the British Minister. Dr Benito is also at the party; he offers William a tour of the country, but William refuses to go. Bannister reveals that the rumour of plague is a lie, circulated to get people out of Jacksonburg.

Section 5

William receives a congratulatory telegram; his contract has been 'unterminated'. Shortly afterwards, Frau Dressler tells him that Kätchen has been arrested by Benito's men. A 'natty young negro' arrives, who says that Dr Benito wishes to examine the specimens of stone that William bought from Kätchen. The milch-goat breaks her rope and sends this 'welter-weight champion' sprawling in the garbage.

Section 6

William drives over to the Consulate with the specimens. They turn out to be gold ore, and Bannister reveals that the Russians have 'bought' Benito and the young Ishmaelite Party.

Section 7

Tea-time in London, discussion of William's possible follow-up.

Section 8

William determined to 'do down' Dr Benito. He sends a two-thousand word cable and goes off alone to Popotakis's.

Section 9

The reception of the cable by Salter and the general editor. His sensational message is carried to two million 'apathetic homes'. Mr Salter returns home convinced of Lord Copper's genius in selecting William for the job.

Section 10

This marks the return of Kätchen's 'husband', who gorges himself on William's complete meal brought from England for Christmas. He reveals that he and others have been helping Smiles Soum, who has absconded to the Sudan. The German then falls asleep. Kätchen arrives, having escaped her captors, and persuades William to pay the taxi-driver's exorbitant charge. She is reunited with her 'husband', and they discuss means of escaping – probably using '*our* boat' (the canoe William had brought from England).

Section 11

William drives through the town with the German couple; Kätchen and her 'husband' set off in the canoe. William goes back; the telegraph boy will not send his cable. William again meets the 'welter-weight champion', who hands him a paper bearing the words 'WORKERS OF ISHMAELIA UNITE'. William sings Uncle Theodore's hymn and prays for the tranquillity of Lush Places. Then an aeroplane swoops down, and a parachutist lands expertly; it turns out to be the mysterious stranger, William's companion on the plane from London on the way to Ishmaelia.

Textual notes, Sections 1–11

Some German friends i.e. some Germans who owed her money.

they have shut him in his bedroom The Nannie-ridden William would have appreciated this; in fact it leads to his scoop.

two black secretaries the hint of a Black Power movement beginning to bid for international status.

milk-bars A popular 1930s type of snack-bar, providing milkshakes, coffee, sandwiches, fruit sundaes etc.

JUNTA A political faction or clique.

Bubonic plague Highly virulent epidemic, marked by inflamed swellings (bubos) in groin and armpit.

like a bloody cemetery Corker is down – and for once cannot bounce back immediately.

divertissement Amusement, treat.

It is all arranged Ominous note being struck, as if William must be got rid of, or at least out of the way.

commercial questionnaires i.e. questions on the country's finances and economics.

a posse Normally associated with Westerns, thus continuing the cinematic technique.

natty Smartly dressed.

the capitulations The terms laid down, on the founding of the state, to protect foreign citizens.

The milch-goat ... kitchen garbage The whole paragraph reflects the triumph of crude nature over supposedly civilized man.

the Mixed Court i.e. consisting of members of nations representing The League of Nations.

out of jug i.e. freed from prison.

to do down i.e. get the better of.

cinematographic consummation The Thirties witnessed many 'colossal' films, and anything about the far-flung British Empire was liable to have Bengal lancers and kilted highlanders thrown in for 'colour'.

like a kitten An unconsciously linked image to Kätchen.

like bristles on a porcupine Fine image to express the reaction of the typewriter to hamfisted treatment.

coup d'état i.e. seizure of power.

It's news ... photograph of Boot The big scene from a dozen films about the newspaper world.

Ovaltine Malted drink of milk and cocoa ingredients, much advertised and consumed in the 1930s.

clipped yew ... neglected garden Again note the economy and visual effect of the image.

five thousand volunteers Equivalent to the numbers of German volunteers in Spain.

the Sudan A large area, then under British control, west of Abyssinia.

Khartoum Capital of the Sudan.

the Matto Grosso A dense forest in Brazil.

I burned out the centre Note the Teutonic thoroughness.

there it was caught Symbolic of William's life at the time.

guichet A small window with a sliding panel, rather like those seen in old-fashioned railway- or theatre-ticket offices.

WORKERS OF ISHMAELIA UNITE The Communist slogan of the time was 'Workers of the World Unite'.

liquidated i.e. wiped out; a phrase that was already becoming ominously familiar in the late 1930s.

Change and decay Indicative of William's life and surroundings, and the state of Ishmaelia itself. But he never needed to echo Uncle Theodore's hymn at Boot Magna.

a god from the machine English translation of the Latin *deus ex machina*: a godlike force that arrives in the nick of time to solve difficulties. Also a dramatic contrivance from the classic theatre, whereby a suffering character is visited by a *god* who offers help, having first been lowered to the stage by *machinery*. (Baldwin's arrival by plane and parachute is the answer to William's prayer for 'a god from the machine'.)

Chapter 5

Section 1

The ending of the first day in Soviet Ishmaelia; William and his mysterious aeroplane companion (now calling himself 'Mr Baldwin'), are in the deserted bar-room of Popotakis's Ping-Pong Parlour. The little man defeats William at ping-pong. Mr Baldwin has a private wireless transmitter, and the bearded ticket-collector is revealed as someone who has worked for Mr Baldwin for a long time. Baldwin reveals that there has been foreign competition for the mineral rights of Ishmaelia, with the Germans supporting Smiles, and the Russians the young Ishmaelite Movement. When the explanations are over, Olafsen appears in search of liquor, to which, in the absence of Popotakis, he helps himself. At the Swede's suggestion, the three set off to visit President Jackson.

When they reach the President's residence, they find Dr Benito in control; the Soviet coup d'état has succeeded. But the drunken Erik Olafsen soon alters this, and the name of Jackson once more resounds to the acclaim of the populace.

William's despatch is expertly written by Baldwin, who describes himself as the 'Mystery Financier' who has secured an 'East African Concession' on behalf of the British. The Jacksons are now restored to power.

Mr Baldwin Waugh's choice of name for this versatile, polyglot 'god from the machine' is a strange one. Stanley Baldwin (1867–1947), the retired Prime Minister, was – with his 'simple countryman' appearance and his ever-present pipe – considered to be a model of rectitude; the kindly honest Englishman of legend.

Love, fifteen Ping-pong, now called table tennis, is not scored in this manner today.

demotic Greek The popular form of modern Greek, as opposed to the more formal language used at the Court or in official and learned publications.

Café Wilberforce A strange reversal – Wilberforce wanted to abolish slavery. (Note Marxville and Café Lenin – after Karl Marx, the founder of Communism, and Lenin, major leader in the Russian revolution of 1917.)

Giraud The name has been borrowed from Henri Giraud (1879–1949), the French general famous in both World Wars.

I plough a lonely furrow I work alone; sounds almost pathetic – except that his real meaning is that no one else gets a cut.

to rough it Waugh's irony, in view of the luxury of the feast.

treasures from the imperial palaces The Russians had not yet learned the true value of the Tzar's art collections (or so Waugh implies) and they had a lot of timber. The Germans had the toys. There is a suggestion here of the contempt both nations felt for the land they hoped to exploit.

Young Ishmaelite Party Reminiscent of the young Turks who were associated with the Germans both before and during World War I.

Pam or Dizzy Lord Palmerston (1784–1865) and Benjamin Disraeli (1804–81); both were forceful Foreign Ministers and Prime Ministers, with pronounced views on the paramount importance of the British Empire.

As he spoke The following two paragraphs give a wonderful impression of what a mild giant can do when he has had enough.

Might Baldwin is pointing the difference between this word and 'force', both used earlier (p.172) by Baldwin; the potential had been there in the Swede all the time, but was only now ready for use.

deep bass, ringing alto A nice suggestion of the balance of power between the two men.

They say they are princes It was a fact that a number of exiled Russians (proverbially waiters or taxi-drivers) were princes; even more 'ennobled' themselves.

ten-hour, ten-day week A nonsensical exaggeration.

the sequence Note again the strong film associations in the book.

locked in the wood shed An association with *Cold Comfort Farm* (1933) by Stella Gibbons – a popular satiric novel, in which there was 'something nasty in the woodshed'.

RHODES LAWRENCE A reference to Cecil Rhodes (1853–1902) the

man who founded Rhodesia (now Zimbabwe), having made a fortune
in South Africa; and T. E. Lawrence (1888–1935), the legendary
Lawrence of Arabia, who harassed the Turks and led the Arabs in
World War I.

Book 3 Banquet

Chapter 1

Section 1

Lord Copper is alone in the Megalopolitan Building; he is joined
by Mr Salter, who reminds him of Boot's triumph in Ishmaelia.
Lord Copper wants a reception for William; he also wants to keep
him in the public eye by providing something new for him to do.
He decides to recommend William for a knighthood, and to hold
a banquet in his honour.

Section 2

The understaffing at 10 Downing Street causes an error, and John
Courteney Boot is informed that he is to be knighted; naturally
he attributes this to Mrs Stitch – whose husband Algernon is
somewhat surprised at the news.

Section 3

William returns to England. He reads what purports to be an article
by him in the *Beast*; he is 'overcome with shame'. He is offered
a number of contracts, but gets rid of them. At Victoria he is met
by young Bateson, but he shakes him off and telegraphs his return
to Boot Magna. Uncle Theodore's welcome is very lukewarm;
William thinks again of his romance with Kätchen in Jacksonburg.

Section 4

William writes to Salter to say that he can't attend the banquet;
Salter is ordered by Lord Copper to get hold of William. Before
he can do so Salter learns of the confusion over the knighthood;

he decides that 'Lord Copper must never know'. Salter then goes down to Boot Magna to reason with William about the banquet.

Textual notes, Sections 1–4

grotto-blue light Daylight lamps were used. The metaphor is from the famous Blue Grotto at Capri, where the light is mysteriously reflected from the sea into the cave.

sub-editor ... misinformation Note the irony of this.

whistling urchins i.e. copy-boys.

rested in sculptural fashion In the manner of Rodin's famous statue *The Thinker*.

an Elgin marble One of a number of Greek sculptures brought to England from Athens by Lord Elgin (1777–1841); they were in danger of being destroyed. They are now in the British Museum.

royals A stag's antlers having twelve or more points.

elegant antennae of the ibis An ibis is a bird; an *ibex* is meant – a type of goat found in Europe's alpine regions.

Bucarest (Usually spelt 'Bucharest' in English); the capital of Romania.

pogrom An organized massacre (as by the Fascists against the Jews in Romania and Poland).

I gave that illiterate fellow He means that he arranged it through the patronage system of the government.

wiped Hitchcock's eye i.e. bested him by taking an advantage that he had missed.

the Lido Famous bathing resort near Venice, after which many open-air swimming pools have been named.

gratis Honours were sometimes given if the recipient had made a contribution to the funds of the ruling party.

with the partridges i.e. shooting.

John Gassoway A good Dickens-type name for an MP.

Overwork i.e. the Prime Minister, not Boot.

Greenidge The name of one of Waugh's friends, an eccentric.

Montesquieu (1689–1753); considered to be the most profound, and the most important, French thinker of the eighteenth century.

ROVING CORRESPONDENT One going almost anywhere he chooses, to write about local conditions.

PLEASE WIRE ... AGENCY Books and serial stories in newspapers and the cinema rights for films of his adventures, all arranged for him, with of course a sum as commission for the literary agent.

on space No regular salary, a fixed sum per column inch that he produced.

Correspondence School One that teaches by lessons sent by post – in this case, for a course in journalism.

balmy Should be 'barmy', meaning 'mad'.

the night's sport i.e. poaching.

On such a night as this The words echo the romantic love of Lorenzo and Jessica in *The Merchant of Venice* – but William's romance has gone.

talking turkey i.e. negotiating.

entourage i.e. those waiting on me, my personal staff.

Household Cavalry This was, then, made up of the Life Guards and the Horse Guards.

I could not consider ... Another knock at the Honours system prevalent at the time; after all, he would possibly have been accused of advancing the Boot family's fortunes at the country's expense.

jobbery Dishonest 'fixing'.

Chapter 2

Section 1

Salter's telegram arrives at Boot Magna; there follows a family discussion of what to do with Salter when he arrives.

Section 2

Salter arrives at Boot Magna – a boy with a horse and cart is there to meet him. It is full of slag, and the youth reveals that as he is a very poor driver he shouldn't be allowed out on his own. Mr Salter decides to walk, and sets out on his way.

Section 3

Salter arrives at the house at eight o'clock, and meets Uncle Theodore. He is so exhausted he collapses and sleeps, and is found by William's mother. James the footman tells Mr Salter of the unfortunate accident to his luggage, which is 'inundated with slag', the farm vehicle bringing it having overturned on its way from the station. Salter finds that he is to stay in Priscilla's room, and that he is to look after Amabel the dog. The family discuss Salter, and consider that he has had too much to drink. At dinner, therefore, they decide to keep the drink away from him. The family conversation and innuendo flow around Mr Salter, but the latter later persuades William to sign a contract with the *Beast*. Still William refuses to attend the banquet, and Mr Salter loses money to Nannie Price. Later he cannot sleep because of the reminiscences of Uncle Theodore, who tries to persuade him to publish them in the *Beast*.

Section 4

Salter reporting back to the *Beast*, Bootless. But another Boot – Uncle Theodore – arrives.

Textual notes, Sections 1–4

For over an hour There are almost as many complications here as on William's journey.

harse Horse.

swole up i.e. distended, swollen.

slag Probably basic slag, a fertilizer prepared at sewage farms.

Westerheys Probably one of the large fields of William's estate: the old names of ploughed fields and meadows still linger today.

durstn't Dare not.

a fair lick A fast rate.

tidy step Fairly long way.

In Thy courts One of Uncle Theodore's hymns.

Hanoverian face i.e. resembling those of the Georges, Kings of Great Britain, 1714–1830.

monocle Single eye-glass.

a rivederci Good-bye for the moment.

loofah The dried fibrous part of the large pod of an African plant, the Dishcloth Gourd (*Luffa cylindrica*), used in the bath as a sponge and back-scrubber.

slots of deer Foot-print or hoof-print. In this case it clearly means (see other souvenirs) the actual hoof.

pads Feet.

all over the shop Everywhere.

squiffy Rather drunk.

sozzled Completely drunk.

Bombay duck A dried Indian fish.

Dijon mustard The best French mustard.

Parmesan cheese Italian cheese, usually grated for a top-dressing.

saltire Heraldic – St Andrew's Cross shape. Uncle Bernard is riding his hobby-horse!

his coat i.e. coat-of-arms.

beyond the Roman pale i.e. outside the Roman sphere of influence.

Heliogabalus (AD 204–22); proclaimed Emperor of Rome, AD 218. He left state affairs to his mother and grandmother, and gave up the rest of his short life to extravagance and depravity.

Willis's rooms A late-night restaurant, specializing in suppers.

Romano's An Italian-run restaurant in the Strand, frequented by the stage/race-course/Bohemian set.

Chapter 3

Section 1

The banquet described, also the guests and Lord Copper. The guest of honour is Uncle Theodore, now elevated – to get everyone out of trouble – to 'Boot of the *Beast*'. Lord Copper has been kept in ignorance of these machinations. The banquet goes on, though it appears that 'Someone had blundered'. Uncle Theodore continues with his lecherous innuendoes, Lord Copper makes his speech in honour of Boot, ending with a toast to the future. The future of all the characters is summarized: Kätchen writes to William for more money for the specimens, and William continues writing his column *Lush Places*.

Textual notes, Section 1

Lord Copper quite often ... interruption A long paragraph of venom directed at Copper.

The old order changeth The famous quotation from *Idylls of the King*: 'The Passing of Arthur', by Alfred, Lord Tennyson (1809–92).

Someone had blundered Tennyson again, this time from the Crimean war poem *The Charge of the Light Brigade*.

Bertie Wodehouse-Bonner A tribute to the brilliant comic writer P. G. Wodehouse (1881–1975), whose main character in the Jeeves stories is Bertie Wooster.

Caesar and Brutus ... Josephine There are two betrayals here: that of Caesar by Brutus; that of Josephine by Napoleon.

monolocution i.e. a discourse monopolized by one person.

inhaling stertorously i.e. loudly snuffing the 'bouquet' (scent) of the brandy.

tropic tide ... foaming surf A continuation of the 'breasting' image, an ironic water image in view of Lord Copper's static person and delivery.

clouded i.e. mottled.

commissionaires Door-keepers, usually uniformed.

amazons Female warriors.

Aegean The Aegean sea lies between Greece and Turkey – the bronzes would probably have come from one of the Greek islands.

Madagascar An island off the African continent.

poste restante Sent to a post office, to be collected.

maternal rodents ... Outside the owls Both William and the predators had a penchant for small furry rodents.

Revision Questions

1 What (and who) are the main objects of Waugh's satire in *Scoop*?

2 Write a character sketch of William. In what ways is he a 'sucker'?

3 Compare and contrast Baldwin and Lord Copper.

4 Write an essay on Waugh's ability to create a particular atmosphere in any part of *Scoop*.

5 In what ways is Waugh a humorous writer? In your answer you should refer to two or three episodes.

6 Justify, by close reference, the sub-title of the novel. 'A novel about journalists'.

7 Do you consider that *Scoop* is a moral book? Give reasons for your answer.

8 In what ways is *Scoop* like a film? In your answer, refer closely to the text.

9 Compare and contrast the Pension Dressler and Boot Magna, bringing out clearly the similarities and the differences.

10 Write a character sketch of Mr Salter. What positive qualities does he possess?

11 Write an essay on Waugh's use of dialogue in *Scoop*.

12 'His is a varied style.' In what ways do you agree or disagree with this comment on Waugh's writing in *Scoop*?

13 What picture of his own times does Waugh give us in *Scoop*?

14 'The structure is somewhat complex'. Discuss this view of *Scoop*.

15 Compare and contrast Mrs Stitch and Kätchen, bringing out clearly the function of each in the novel.

16 Estimate the contribution to the humour of the novel made by Uncle Theodore and Erik Olafsen.

17 In what ways do you consider that Waugh relies on the grotesque for his effects?

18 'Profoundly cynical.' How far would you agree with this comment on *Scoop*?

19 Consider the parts the journalists play in the novel, indicating whether you think there is anything redeeming in their behaviour.

20 Write an essay on Waugh's use of mistaken identity in *Scoop*.